E-sports

Making Sense of Complexity in Technology

(A Guide to Launching Your Career in the Exciting World of Esports)

Michael Cummins

Published By **Cathy Nedrow**

Michael Cummins

E-sports: Making Sense of Complexity in Technology (A Guide to Launching Your Career in the Exciting World of Esports)

ISBN 978-1-9990334-9-1

No part of this guidebook shall be reproduced in any form without permission in writing from the publisher except in the case of brief quotations embodied in critical articles or reviews.

Legal & Disclaimer

The information contained in this book is not designed to replace or take the place of any form of medicine or professional medical advice. The information in this book has been provided for educational & entertainment purposes only.

The information contained in this book has been compiled from sources deemed reliable, and it is accurate to the best of the Author's knowledge; however, the Author cannot guarantee its accuracy and validity and cannot be held liable for any errors or omissions. Changes are periodically made to this book. You must consult your doctor or get professional medical advice before using any of the suggested remedies, techniques, or information in this book.

Upon using the information contained in this book, you agree to hold harmless the Author from and against any damages, costs, and expenses, including any legal fees potentially resulting from the application of any of the information provided by this guide. This disclaimer applies to any damages or injury caused by the use and application, whether directly or indirectly, of any advice or information presented, whether for breach of contract, tort, negligence, personal injury, criminal intent, or under any other cause of action.

You agree to accept all risks of using the information presented inside this book. You need to consult a professional medical practitioner in order to ensure you are both able and healthy enough to participate in this program.

Table Of Contents

Chapter 1: Nutritional Challenges in Gaming

Good nutrients within the gaming and esports surroundings face some stressful situations. Just with the resource of visiting network region networks (LAN) or esports activities, you may normally see numerous fast-food eating places and power drink shops. Some of these foods and drinks items look like fed on at a better rate with the aid of gamers and esports athletes than the relaxation of the population. A present day examine on youngsters in Norway depicts an extended consumption of energy drinks in youngsters with advanced display display time and coffee physical interest (12). Also, there seems to be a correlation among digital device usage and caffeine and sugar intake, with the possibility of exceeding the sugar- and caffeine-consumption guidelines through seven and four percentage, respectively, with every more hour of video game use(13). Another modern-day take a look at published in 2018 reports a robust association with a decrease intake of end result and greens and an accelerated intake of each speedy-food and sugar-sweetened drinks (SSB), with accelerated time spent gambling digital games (14). Lipsky et al. Stated that better weight loss plan excellent became visible in emerging adults taking component in not unusual physical interest, breakfasts, and circle of relatives food, at the equal time as inversely associated with gaming and the use of different virtual media (15). Finally, a check posted in the American Journal of Clinical Nutrition in 2014 shows that extended show time is related to the intake of meals with low nutritional tremendous (i.E., SSBs, goodies, speedy-meals, and salty snacks)(16).

Energy drinks have been within the gaming network for many years. In the gaming and esports company, there are a few claimed blessings of ingesting strength drinks for gamers. The problem with this is that the scientific literature at the overall performance-improving problem can be very scarce. Currently, there can be best one have a check that has looked at the overall performance of esports athletes and the intake of power drinks(17). This have a look at did not show any overall performance-improving impact on both cognitive or physical common performance. However, greater research are wished on gamers and esports athletes to assess the impact of caffeine-rich products on general usual overall performance.

There is little studies on why the ones merchandise are so large within the gaming community. However, I firmly receive as actual with there are multiple reasons for this. First of all, the products incorporate caffeine, which has some documented results on cognitive normal overall performance. Also, the ones beverages can delay sleep due to the results of caffeine, so that you can supply gamers extra up-time on close by vicinity community sports(6; 7; 18). On pinnacle of this, the electricity beverages encompass severa vitamins and minerals, which may be said to decorate cognitive function similarly. This effect of vitamins and minerals on cognitive general overall performance is, but, quite debatable, and the medical proof for this announcement is scarce at excellent.

Manufacturers of products inclusive of Red Bull and Monster are deeply invested within the esports scene, sponsoring top gamers, agencies, and occasions anywhere inside the global. These sponsorships create a strong brand presence, apparent to each new and contemporary-day gamers and spectators(19). The brand presence is even in addition greater while the usage of modern influencers, which consist of the most big streamers and YouTubers in the world, to promote particular merchandise.

In the previous couple of years, greater location of interest products have arrived, focused on gamers and esports athletes even further. Some of the greater famous names are G-Fuel, Gamer Supps, and Rogue Energy. G-Fuel, claiming to be the reliable drink of esports(20), includes even more materials than the normal energy drinks which consist of Red Bull or Monster. It carries quite huge doses of different vitamins and minerals. The G-Fuel "power complex" includes quite a few distinct substances, beginning from nutrients and minerals to ergogenic aids which encompass L-citrulline malate and caffeine. One of these vitamins, vitamins B12, portions to 17,708% of the every day cost primarily based totally on a 2,000-calorie food regimen(21). This is a big dose of food regimen B12, and there can be presently no evidence that lets in any cognitive performance-enhancing effect above the ordinary nutrients B12 reputation(22; 23; 24). A regular nutrition B12 popularity can be acquired thru using eating meat, fish, seafood, eggs, and dairy merchandise. Since most of those nutrients and minerals are ingested sufficiently in a healthful and balanced diet plan, it's vain to complement via such electricity beverages. A particular analogy is to pour water into a tumbler, representing supplementing with food regimen B12. When the glass is full, you have reached the maximum effect of that vitamin. If you continue to pour water into the glass, it's going to genuinely spill over and be wasted, or in the case of weight loss program B12, be excreted in the urine.

The best ability overall performance-enhancer for game enthusiasts in those energy drinks is caffeine. However, an excessive amount of caffeine will inhibit cognitive characteristic, further to yielding several certainly one of a kind element effects collectively with cardiac and gastrointestinal troubles(6; 7). Caffeinated electricity liquids in powder shape, which includes G-Fuel, also can increase the danger of overdosing on caffeine, compared to everyday energy beverages. This is because of the fact the character can determine the dosage of caffeine themselves, in desire to consuming a pre-mixed electricity drink from the producer. On top of this, there are high-quality capacity facet-results associated with electricity drinks, which encompass chance-attempting to find behaviors and dental problems(25).

There are likely numerous elements contributing to the increased intake of caffeine, power beverages, SSBs, and, in popular, meals with low dietary super. First of all, I bear in mind that dietary literacy is exceptionally low within the gaming network. In my opinion, there does not seem like a big interest in vitamins as a health or not unusual average overall performance-enhancing detail. Also, there can be heavy branding in this community from fast-food and power drink manufacturers. Finally, energy drinks have already got a sturdy records and function inside the gaming life-style, which I consider makes it less tough to keep selling those merchandise with an lousy lot lots much less resistance from the clients.

THE BASICS OF PRACTICAL NUTRITION WORK

There are numerous elements to preserve in mind at the same time as discussing healthy and regular performance-enhancing diets. First of all, getting all the essential nutrients and minerals from virtually considered one of a kind meals compounds is essential for real fitness and ordinary performance. Also, ingesting sufficient strength to cover the each day electricity requirements is important. Factors like dietary supplementation and the use of regular overall performance-improving dietary dietary supplements are the pinnacle of the overall typical overall performance pyramid – they may be capable of most effective supply a minor improve in overall performance. That is why the primary interest should be at the basics of vitamins, together with ingesting nice food, on account that this could offer you with "the most bang in your dollar."

Figure 1. This version is a instance of different factors influencing in-hobby overall performance for an esports athlete from a nutritional mindset. At the lowest of the pyramid, maximum of the overall usual overall performance is received. Elements which incorporates gambling the game, studying fighters, and developing strategies for you or your organization are the inspiration. At the following degree, distinct factors that can have an impact on standard overall performance at a lower charge come into play, which encompass eating regimen, bodily education, and highbrow schooling. Finally, only some levels of ordinary overall performance can be received with, for instance, nutritional dietary supplements.

Chapter 2: Caloric Estimations

An thrilling question which I am requested once in a while is "How many energy do I want a day?" The quantity of meals and calories one goals regular with day is predicated upon on several elements, and the manner of estimating with a diploma of reality is tremendously medical. If you want a "brief repair" on figuring out each day caloric desires, you may find out this at the save you of this phase, or in my preceding ebook, "A Theoretical Guide to Esports Nutrition."

The maximum accurate approach is the use of a manner known as doubly categorized water (DLW). The approach of the use of DLW can be very price- and time-consuming and is seldom used in practical nutrients art work. The 2d technique, this is used by most practitioners, is primarily based on equations estimating the caloric consumption. This method is called the factorial approach, in which the resting power expenditure (REE), moreover referred to as the resting metabolic charge (RMR), is advanced through a detail indicating physical interest degree (PAL). These prediction equations aren't as accurate as DLW, but the factorial method offers an opportunity to generalize the effects. The desk below illustrates the equations for 2 one in every of a type age companies of adults (each male and woman), as provided in Nordic Nutrition Recommendations 2012(24).

Table 1. Equations extrapolated from Nordic Nutrition Recommendations 2012. The equations used for estimating not unusual resting metabolic charge (RMR) in megajoules (MJ) based on every weight (W, kg) or weight and top (H, m)(24).

For the sake of simplicity, I will keep to discuss the ones examples in kcal, at the grounds that in my enjoy game enthusiasts and esports athletes are extra used to working with kcal in preference to MJ. Estimating the RMR for a 21-12 months-old male who weighs 70 kilos will appear to be this: 0,0669 prolonged thru 70 plus 2,28, it is 6,963. The expected RMR is 6,963 MJ/day, that is the same as 1663 kilocalories (kcal). This conversion from MJ to kcal is based at the price of one kilojoule to 0,24 kcal(24). The RMR we've got got honestly calculated is the power the 21-yr-vintage male wishes in keeping with day to preserve the structures of the frame in addition to regulating the frame temperature at relaxation. The RMR is likewise based totally totally on a temperature-managed surroundings (no longer too warmness or too cold) and no bodily interest(26). To find out an estimate for the overall energy desired according to day, we want to embody sports activities together with physical exercise, consuming, and operating. These PAL values, as noted in advance, are based on research the use of DLW, and the overall calories desired in keeping with day are a made of RMR and PAL. This caloric need can variety masses counting on the every day sports activities. For instance, a marathon runner training for 3 hours an afternoon will expend plenty extra strength than an place of business worker. Below is a table illustrating the specific PAL values from NNR 2012(24) based totally at the have a study by way of way of using Black et al. On strength expenditure using DLW(27).

Table 2. Physical hobby diploma (PAL) values from one-of-a-kind activities. Leisure pastime can encompass brisk taking walks, on the equal time as exertive art work or athletic education can encompass going for walks.

However, to get a better estimate of the PAL charge, one has to summarize all of the sports activities for someday (24 hours) with wonderful metabolic same values. The considered one of a kind values for the depth of hobby (MET) are as follows: relaxation 1,zero, very mild 1,5, moderate 2,zero, mild 5,zero, and strenuous 10,0(24). For instance, for the duration of an afternoon with ten hours of gaming, the intensity of this interest might be considered very light. With eight hours of sleep, we've six hours left of the day. The remaining six hours of the day is probably considered as mild pastime, with sports activities collectively with meals prep, consuming, a few workplace paintings, and so forth. Table three illustrates this case, further to calculating the PAL charge on the quit.

Table three. To estimate a PAL fee, a few calculations are preferred. The intensity of activities for the duration of the day is increased by means of manner of the usage of the kind of hours spent in the ones one-of-a-kind sports. Finally, that is divided through 24 to get the common price, which represents the PAL fee used to estimate the each day caloric desires. The instance in this table is of a gamer with a very sedentary life-style and no physical schooling.

Let us look at each distinct example, an esports athlete with the equal amount of gaming in keeping with day however with hours of workout as well. These athletes may additionally, in some instances, get their meals organized for them, and their primary paintings is playing esports. So, for simplicity, allow us to assume we're capable of switch out hours of mild hobby with hours of strenuous workout. This instance is hooked up in desk four.

Table four. To estimate an appropriate PAL fee, the intensity of sports activities throughout the day is increased through the sizeable form of hours spent in those precise sports. Finally, this is divided through 24 to get the common rate, which represents the PAL fee used to estimate the every day caloric goals. This instance is of an esports athlete with hours of strenuous physical pastime.

As validated in tables 3 and four, the difference within the PAL values is massive (1,46 instead of 2,13). To estimate the every day desires of kcal consistent with day, allow us to apply the earlier instance of the 21-12 months-antique male weighing 70 kg, with an RMR of 1663 kcal. In the number one example, without a strenuous activity, the kcal wished in line with day to stay weight-sturdy might be 1663 advanced via 1,46, which equals 2428 kcal consistent with day. If we use the second instance, with hours of strenuous interest, we get the subsequent result: 1663 accelerated via 2,13, which equals 3542 kcal in line with day, to preserve a strong weight. That is form of 1000 kcal difference in keeping with day simply because of the strenuous bodily interest. If you need to do a more honest calculation, however with masses much less precision, the not unusual PAL rate in the Nordic countries is expected at 1,6(24).

After going through this certain rationalization of the way to calculate the expected electricity requirements regular with day — do athletes plan their food every day in this element? It may be used as a device to get a top level view of the quantity of food and energy wanted constant with day to attain a cause. Still, in my enjoy, very few athletes weigh their food every day to reap a selected caloric motive. Measuring meals may be of sensible use for athletes in search of to learn how to estimate the caloric content cloth material of food clearly measuring with the useful resource of eye, but it isn't always regularly used on a every day basis. It may be very time-ingesting and power-draining to weigh each meals item of each meal. It is likewise very impractical at the same time as you're visiting 2 hundred days or extra sooner or later of a yr. It is critical for each athlete to discover about vitamins so modifications can be made at the pass.

If the goal is to modify body weight, it may be realistic to use a frame weight scale to tune progression and regulate the meals and power based totally totally on that improvement. For instance, if an athlete desires to lessen weight however weighs the equal more than one weeks in a row, an answer may be to lessen on a meal or .

The meals and calorie reduction want to, but, be expected to possibly 250 to 500 energy in deficit, so having an idea of ways a good buy food that permits you to quantity to is crucial. Nevertheless, there are instances in which this approach will not work. In the ones scenarios, it is probably due to illnesses, metabolic disturbances or fantastic physiological elements.

The component is that every day the interest stage changes, which makes the power requirements change. It is tough to control the precise range of electricity one expends, further to the proper range of electricity to ingest. If the motive is weight-regulation, it is also extra available to base it on the present day food regimen of the athlete with some modifications and display the weight weekly. The technique cited in advance in this economic catastrophe have to be a useful guiding principle to estimate the each day caloric desires, but that is all it's far.

NUTRITIONAL QUALITY

Different meals objects provide one of a kind nutritional content material cloth. For example, a frozen pizza and an apple have precise micro- and macronutrient compositions. In regular lifestyles, it's miles critical to eat healthy and nutritious food for numerous reasons. Our our our our bodies need to achieve the endorsed portions of nutrients and minerals from our diets. Most of those nutrients and minerals are crucial for particular techniques in the body, collectively with mobile proliferation and differentiation(28), eye-sight(29), and brain characteristic(30). Also, wholesome meals include other bioactive compounds vital for famous properly-being and the prevention of diseases, e.G., cardiovascular ailment and most cancers(31). These compounds are not a few aspect you could resultseasily alternative via dietary dietary supplements.

The following desk summarizes the recommended every day consumption of different micronutrients for the not unusual adult male and female populace, based totally on the Nordic Nutrition Recommendations 2012(24):

Table five. This desk indicates the advocated each day intake of

one-of-a-type micronutrients for adults, from the Nordic Nutrition Recommendations 2012.

*Vitamin D pointers are for 2 to seventy 4 years of age. For seventy five years and older, the encouraged intake is 20 µg in line with day.

1For ladies of reproductive age, the advice is 4 hundred µg in line with day.

2For post-menopausal girls, the advice is 9 mg steady with day.

It is beneficial to get the endorsed consumption of these micronutrients via food, and this is commonly no longer a hassle in case you are consuming enough and a various weight loss program. Different food gadgets include various quantities of vitamins and minerals, ultimately the importance of numerous meals consumption. However, there are a few nutrients and minerals that may be difficult to gain in most first-class dosages through a numerous food plan. An instance of this is nutrition D. Vitamin D is on the entire synthesized within the pores and pores and skin because of UVB radiation from daytime publicity. This may be complicated for a few religions, in which the clothing hides most of the pores and pores and pores and skin. It is likewise a hassle in nations above a outstanding variety, because the solar rays will no longer acquire the pores and pores and skin to synthesize weight-reduction plan D sufficiently(32). Consequently, many people the world over are nutrition D poor(33). In the ones eventualities, it is probably relevant to get a medical assessment of the nutrition D popularity to supplement with the proper dosages of the food regimen. You ought to not complement with one-of-a-kind vitamins and minerals until you're horrific. This is critical, specially for fats-soluble vitamins, as they will, in excessive dosages, have component effects(34).

The advocated kind of vitamins and minerals will typically be sufficient for best fitness and ordinary universal performance. There is currently no massive proof to manual nutritional dietary dietary dietary supplements that growth your food regimen and mineral popularity above the encouraged guidelines, in phrases of each health or overall performance. This makes ingesting multivitamins and minerals pointless in case you already consume a balanced weight-reduction plan with enough micronutrients.

Chapter 3: Nutritional Composition

Eating the right quantity of various electricity assets is essential for fitness and fundamental ordinary performance. Also, the ratio between protein, carbohydrate, and fat within the eating regimen will show, to a high-quality degree, the content fabric cloth of micronutrients. Eating a diet plan with 80% of the caloric consumption received from low-best carbohydrates, which includes snacks, chocolate, sodas, and candy, shows a weight loss plan rich in sugars. On the opportunity hand, eating a diet with 20% of the each day caloric consumption obtained from carbohydrates may also additionally suggest a low fiber intake, in addition to depleted glycogen stores, depending on the bodily interest diploma of the individual. The table underneath gives a hard estimate of the special macronutrients for a normal gamer or esports athlete with little to no bodily interest. These guidelines will help to ensure that the character gets crucial nutritional elements, along with nutrients, minerals, fiber, and vital fatty acids (24).

Table 6. This table represents the precept tips for macronutrient intake for the common population(24). These recommendations need to be appropriate for maximum esports athletes as properly.

The dietary examples on this ebook will use the pointers in this monetary wreck for each macro- and micronutrients. Subpopulations consisting of conventional athletes or humans with unique dietary desires will need to alter their weight loss program accordingly.

The macronutrient composition of food inside the path of the day can variety. For example, earlier than an excessive exercising, consuming a meal wealthy in carbohydrates and a mild in protein might be more beneficial for the digestion than a meal rich in saturated fat, fiber, and distinct components that make food skip greater slowly through the digestive tract. A meal that takes a long time to digest may additionally deliver a gastrointestinal problem if an excessive workout is completed fast after the meal. However, in latest, slowly digested food are maximum green, because those meals help preserve the blood sugar regulated. It has been well set up that glycemic manage is crucial in each preventing and delaying the improvement of diabetes-related complications(35). Also, for gamers and esports athletes, having nicely-regulated blood sugar is vital for pinnacle-great cognitive overall performance(1).

SUMMARY

The following elements summarize the vital detail messages in this section:

Estimating your caloric wishes might probable give you a better assessment of ways a good buy and what you could devour. It can be performed both by using a median PAL rate or through calculating all of your sports activities in a few unspecified time inside the destiny of the day to get a more unique estimate. However, recollect that the ones calculations are exceptional estimates.

Make sure you devour awesome food. Nutrient-dense food gadgets are normally the super possibility for health and overall performance as they incorporate extra nutrients and minerals.

Try to eat a balanced food plan, with 10-20% of your power from protein, forty five-60% from carbohydrates, and 20-35% from fat. This will make sure you get essential nutrients and minerals from every macronutrient employer, as long as you choose superb meals gadgets interior each organisation. Athletes or human beings with ailments may want to probably want to adjust their intake of those macronutrients.

MEAL PLANNING

You have now determined out approximately important subject matters – or what I could probable call gear – that you may observe in your nutrition. Planning your diet plan is critical, in particular if you are journeying, competing or have a very good time table with few breaks. My advice is which you create a "framework" to your nutrients, beginning with at the same time as and the manner regularly you consume at some point of an afternoon. You can also make weekly plans, counting on how that fits it slow desk. Many athletes have an unpredictable weekly time desk and find out it tough to devise for a whole week at a time. There also appear to be institutions among meal making plans and a more suit healthy dietweight-reduction plan with a first rate deal a whole lot less weight issues(36), which type of makes experience as well.

MEAL FREQUENCY AND TIMING

How many food you eat at some level in the day may be of significance for each fitness and normal overall performance. In the literature, there are conflicting effects concerning the effect of meal frequency on the overall fitness, body composition, and well-being of the not unusual populace(37; 38; 39; forty). This is in comparison to what many keep in mind: that a higher meal frequency will, thru using itself, assist with weight regulation. What many human beings could likely overlook at the same time as discussing weight-law is that it is, in principle, a mathematical equation, as we've got were given stated in in advance chapters. For example, if the purpose is to shed pounds, it does now not rely whether or not one eats three or six food regular with day so long as there may be a caloric deficit(forty one; forty two). However, keep in thoughts that this pleasant debts for the goal of weight loss. Other critical elements, consisting of how meal frequency influences cognitive trendy overall performance, are an awful lot less studied. It has been mounted that meals great does have an impact on cognitive capability and that greater wholesome meals are better for cognitive general performance(40 three). Adjusting meal frequency additionally can be of importance in case you are doing sports activities activities or different bodily demanding duties regularly.

You want to tailor the diet regime for your desires. Meal making plans is probably a amazing difficulty if you have a completely prolonged gaming consultation ahead of you. If you aren't eating for numerous hours at the same time as in the center of a gaming consultation, it'd make you hungry and take the point of interest faraway from your gaming overall performance. Planning to have healthy snacks whilst you play, or timing your food so you consume near your gaming consultation, is probably viable techniques to preserve cognitive performance. Another state of affairs is a gamer or an esports athlete who moreover enjoys rigorous energy education and wants to construct muscle corporations. In this situation, it's miles critical for finest muscle protein synthesis (MPS) to be in a caloric surplus, similarly to ingesting protein-rich food a piece greater frequently, in all likelihood every three to 4 hours, with at the least 4 food regular with day(forty four). The table under illustrates examples on specific days, and methods to in shape in meals throughout these days relying on one-of-a-type styles of sports sports.

Table 7. The table illustrates extraordinary examples of each day sports, with approximate schedules for amazing food and snacks in keeping with day. Notice that the hours among the meals generally range from three to 4 hours. Often ready approximately one hour (or extra if needed) earlier than exercising after a meal is beneficial due to viable stomach ache.

This desk is meant to be an concept at the way to schedule your days. Concerning the day with four food, as you could see, there aren't any snack food. During in recent times, there are numerous lengthy breaks wherein it is viable to consume right meals. Therefore, there may be no need to ingest snack food. On the day with five meals, there may be one snack meal ate up earlier than lunch. This is because of the reality there are nearly six hours amongst breakfast and lunch. The time table does not want to be exactly in line with the times represented in the desk, but word how there are among 3 and 4 hours amongst each meal. This instance is a tough outline of ways to devise meals round one of a kind sports. It moreover can be treasured to time table in breaks some of the gaming periods so you can maintain awesome and awareness at the gameplay. Finally, it's far critical to get enough sleep. For the average man or woman, aiming for about seven to 9 hours of sleep constant with day guarantees superior fitness benefits(forty five).

IMPORTANT MEALS DURING THE DAY

BREAKFAST

Breakfast is frequently provided as one of the most vital food of the day. However, this will in all likelihood rely on different factors. For example, in case you are doing an interest that calls for fine cognitive overall performance, together with a gaming session, breakfast seems to beautify cognition. This association is more potent whilst the diet regime is low in nutritional high-quality and amount(46; 47; 48; 49). There also are sturdy institutions between skipping breakfast and terrible nutrients terrific within the diet(50). In summary, which means that skipping breakfast may be very lousy for the nutritional exceptional of your food plan.

Breakfast composition can range depending on the sports for the relaxation of the day. If there can be an upcoming physical education consultation within the morning (in particular, patience education), breakfast have to frequently consist of carbohydrates to keep away from glycogen depletion at some point of the exercising. It is critical to preserve euglycemia because of the mind's need for glycogen. If you have were given troubles eating breakfast pre-workout, or your urge for food is low, an outstanding technique may be to ingest carbohydrates during workout. This technique can assist to keep live glycogen shops further to booking glycogen shops in muscle fibers(51). The omission of breakfast may also create a terrible power stability inside the path of the day. Skipping this meal can be counter-green for athletes having quite a few physical training or if the reason is to increase weight(fifty two). If it's miles a energy training session, a superb amount of protein additionally may be beneficial for ultimate muscle protein synthesis. It will even make contributions to the each day protein intake.

LUNCH

Lunch is typically the principle meal among breakfast and dinner. Considering breakfast and dinner is probably many hours aside, it is generally clever to have lunch to preserve the blood sugar robust to hold general standard performance. In my opinion, lunch can frequently be very nutritious, relying at the meal. For the ones of you that have warm food blanketed on your art work lunch, this meal may also often be similar to dinner. If it resembles a dinner meal, the meal can be dense in awesome nutrients, with pretty a few greens and nutritious meals gadgets. Having lunch additionally can be of importance because of the harm it gives from art work, college, gaming or a few other hobby. Rest is needed to hold notable overall performance and preserve your interest up. There is likewise an association amongst consuming lunch and better nutrients first rate within the weight loss program(50).

DINNER

For lots of humans, dinner is the most important meal of the day(fifty 3; fifty four). If the cause is to stay weight-stable, it isn't always a hassle if this meal is greater than the others. For many humans, a large dinner may be big because of nutrient content material, specially if the meal earlier than dinner is of terrible dietary super. For instance, youth or teens could probable need to installation their food inside the route of the day, on the same time as the parents make dinner. In my experience, the meals the parents make are often extra nutritious than meals those greater younger boys and girls installation on their personal. These dinner food may additionally moreover furthermore variety masses, which permits with dietary range inside the food plan.

Chapter 4: Meal Plan Examples

This segment will encompass examples of meal plans with precise caloric content material. These meal plans are meant most effective as an suggestion and are not tailored for a selected reason. Hence, the reference values for macronutrient distribution are adjusted for the non-athletic population and are listed as opportunities. For athletes competing in persistence sports activities sports, the pointers for carbohydrates are based totally mostly on grams in keeping with kilo body weight, not probabilities. This additionally applies to power athletes concerning the protein consumption steady with day, wherein the recommendations are based totally absolutely mostly on grams in line with kilo frame weight. Currently, there are not any guidelines for esports athletes as a populace. Esports athletes are running towards for five to 10 hours an afternoon or more, mainly in schooling for competitions(57). Most in all likelihood, that is consultant for maximum days outside of suits for the pleasant esports athletes. Practicing to play on the top degree calls for is lots of sitting, and the physical desires are low. So, besides there can be bodily schooling outside of the gaming, the PAL fee is maximum possibly low. This, in flip, way that the general energy name for for esports athletes is low, probable on the same degree due to the truth the commonplace population with low bodily interest stages.

Variations within the food plan are vital. Therefore, eating the identical meal plan again and again once more could probably purpose sub-top of the line health and preferred standard overall performance. The meal plan must be tailor-made for your needs. If you want to strive a meal plan, it is able to be clever first of all developing a goal (e.G., weight reduction, surely optimizing the dietary first-rate or possibly weight advantage), then maintain to estimate your each day energy expenditure. Finally, growing and the usage of a meal plan permit you to acquire the dreams you have were given set. Using experts that will help you layout a meal plan tailored to you and your desires is crucial for most pleasing results.

The following meal plans all obtain the encouraged every day consumption for each women and men of the brilliant micronutrients indexed in table 5, besides for cases with precise dreams (pregnancy, illnesses or clinical deficiencies). For a healthful character, the ones plans should deliver the micronutrients needed for tremendous fitness and performance. However, numerous factors have an impact on the micronutrient content material material within the ones food objects. These factors are, as an instance, the soil, food animals eat, time of harvest, transportation, processing, and strategies of assessment(fifty eight; fifty nine). These variety from u.S. To united states of america of the usa, and the values furnished within the meal plans in this section are derived from the Norwegian "Matvaretabellen"(60), which suggests the micro- and macronutrient content material material material of numerous thousand food gadgets. The nutritional values want to now not be interpreted as unique values however as an alternative as a representative degree for the micronutrients. Usually, this rate is a mean or a mean internal a diploma of variant(58). The software program software used to plot in the food gadgets, further to doing the calculations for electricity and micro- and macronutrients, is called "Dietist"(sixty one).

2000 KCAL DAILY MEAL PLAN EXAMPLE

The following 2000 kcal meal plan is an normal example of a "clean" (little added sugar, low on trans- and saturated fat, and espresso sodium content) meal plan. Most of the meals gadgets are commonplace in Nordic nations. The meal plan is currently divided into 5 meals. However, if you need to interrupt up it into four meals, it's far possible to increase the scale of four of the food at the same time as eliminating the fifth meal. In that way, the energy may be the same. The supper meal may be used as a snack or in-among meal, and it's far viable to exchange the meals round at some degree within the day.

Table eight. This table illustrates a each day meal plan containing approximately 2000 kilocalories. The plan additionally includes the advocated every day consumption of the micronutrients listed with values within the Nordic Nutrition

Recommendations 2012, besides for humans looking expanded portions because of illnesses, pregnancy or unique precise instances. The plan does not don't forget food allergies or intolerances. The nutritional fiber consumption is prepared 33 grams, this is inside the minimal endorsed range for adults. Added sugars are also below the recommended threshold of 10% of ordinary every day energy consumption(24). The values are based on common or median values. This plan has approximately the subsequent macronutrient distribution of the entire every day electricity intake: 20% protein, 31% fat, and 49% carbohydrates (carbohydrates encompass fiber). All quantities of the meals devices listed in the desk are pre-cooked (of their raw form).

2500 KCAL DAILY MEAL PLAN EXAMPLE

This meal plan containing approximately 2500 kcal illustrates how you may incorporate six food/snacks at some point of the day. There are four primary meals and snack food. The snack food are smaller in every period and calories than the 4 vital food. A meal plan which incorporates six meals might be beneficial for prolonged days, as an example, a event day which begins early within the morning and ends late in the night time. It is possible to merge food if crucial. Combining every the snack food will bring about a meal that has approximately the equal kilocalories as the alternative four food.

Table 9. This desk illustrates a each day meal plan containing about 2500 kilocalories. The plan additionally consists of the advocated each day consumption of the micronutrients indexed with values in the Nordic Nutrition Recommendations

2012, except for people desiring advanced amounts because of ailments, being pregnant, or different specific events. The plan does not recall food allergies or intolerances. The nutritional fiber intake is about forty five grams, this is above the minimum encouraged range for adults. Added sugars also are under the advocated threshold of 10% of ordinary every day electricity intake(24). The values are based on average or median values. This plan has approximately the subsequent macronutrient distribution of the overall day by day energy consumption: sixteen.Five% protein, 34,6% fat, and 48,nine% carbohydrates. All quantities of the meals items indexed within the table are pre-cooked (of their uncooked shape).

3000 KCAL DAILY MEAL PLAN EXAMPLE

This plan has 4 vital food and snack meals. It is possible to combine both snack meals into one meal. In this plan, I in truth have described the kind of meal, to avoid confusion. For example, the additives used in the first snack meal are applicable to a smoothie. The identical for the supper meal (porridge); in case you sincerely mixed the ones additives in a bowl, they will now not flavor as real.

Table 10. This table illustrates a each day meal plan containing approximately 3000 kilocalories. The plan moreover consists of the advocated each day intake of the micronutrients listed with values within the Nordic Nutrition Recommendations 2012, besides for people desiring advanced amounts because of illnesses, being pregnant, or different particular conditions. The plan does now not take into account food hypersensitive reactions or intolerances. The nutritional fiber intake is set fifty two grams, that is above the minimum advocated variety for adults.

Added sugars are also below the advocated threshold of 10% of stylish each day energy intake(24). The values are primarily based mostly on common or median values. This plan has approximately the following macronutrient distribution of the full every day electricity intake: 18,4% protein, 29,9% fat, and fifty one,6% carbohydrates. All portions of the food gadgets indexed within the desk are pre-cooked (in their raw form).

MEAL PREP

THE BASICS STEPS OF MEAL PREP

Meal prep is based totally absolutely mostly on making prepared numerous complete meals so you can simply take one out and warmth it (or devour it bloodless) every time you need to. There are institutions among humans spending time on getting ready meals and better diet regime great, for instance, a higher intake of fruits and veggies(sixty two). Meal prepping is also some difficulty which could shop whenever and cash. It calls for a few planning, collectively with ensuring you've got were given sufficient additives to your deliberate food. When you've got got all of the factors prepared, you keep time via cooking as soon as, rather than doing this technique numerous instances.

STEP I: THE PLANNING

It does not depend whether or not you are a expert chef or green within the kitchen; you could continuously put together some meals that you revel in at your capabilities stage. The meal prepping does not have to be advanced, and you may gain fantastic and nutritious meals while no longer having the capacity of a chef. It additionally can be meals this is quality loved bloodless, so that you do now not want to fear approximately it being a "dinner meal" that desires to be warm to enjoy. The meals can be a few component from sandwiches to dinner-like meals along with fowl, rice, and vegetables. What is critical is which you format the meals to be balanced and nutritious. For maximum human beings, this will be a deliver of carbohydrates, proteins, and fat a great way to assist to ensure a balance inside the macronutrients. Also, having part of greens is important in getting vitamins and minerals. However, the kind of various macronutrients will want to be tailor-made to each man or woman, in step with their very own desires. As stated in advance, the wide sort of carbohydrates, proteins, and fats and the quantity of food in keeping with meal can variety highly counting on the motive this is set.

When the form of meal is planned, the following problem to do is break up it up into the wonderful additives and write a buying list. Some people may also need to have a charge variety in advance than going shopping for, counting on financial flexibility. Having a restriction on the amount of cash you use on the meal prep can be smart, so you need to choose out a number of the inexpensive meals objects (as long as this does not compromise too much on great). Pay hobby to sales on food gadgets you generally consume. Food objects with prolonged expiration dates or that may be frozen may be offered in bulk to shop cash. Just be aware that some food items have to now not be frozen within the occasion that they have been frozen already, as an example, meat and fish. I advise studying the meals labeling for facts approximately the product you are shopping for. Usually, it states whether or not or now not it's been frozen or no longer. Reading the label may even help you apprehend the dietary content material cloth of the meals devices. On the ingredients label, the elements are listed in a hierarchical order. This method that the element there may be most of inside the product is listed first. This will assist you have a look at merchandise to each wonderful, in addition to comparing whether or not or not the meals item is of a first rate nutritional fantastic. For instance, if you have meat products of the same type, you could have a test the label to find out which of the products contains the maximum meat (normally labeled as a percent, e.G., 86% ground pork, or ninety two% hen).

Calculating the constant with-meal charge can be interesting in case you need to compare the meal prices and find out which of your meal preps are the cheapest. Calculate the approximate rate of your wellknown elements earlier than shopping for and divide it through using the type of food. If you don't have any concept of the cost of the factors, make an estimate whilst you are purchasing. Write it down and hold it in a list for the destiny, as it may be thrilling to have a look at the fees of the specific food you have become organized.

Before you buy groceries, ensure you've got were given sufficient area in your refrigerator and freezer to hold your food items. It can be realistic to schedule shopping for precise days or hours to bypass ability queues in the shop, which saves hundreds of time. Also, there might be extra food objects available, in particular if you plan your looking for at the same time as the grocery shop gets its transport.

Step I key factors:

Plan your meals for each meal prep

Choose wholesome meals gadgets on your plan

Make a grocery list

Make splendid you have got had been given space within the refrigerator

THE SHOPPING

The shopping for is commonly the clean element, at least when you have completed step one. The first important thing, in my view, is not to move grocery buying when hungry. This could probable result in horrific meals options and more money spent on needless meals items. Make positive you consume a splendid meal earlier than going shopping for, as shopping in large portions can take some time.

Chapter 5: Expiration Dates and Earnings

Hygiene can be very vital while cooking, so wash your fingers and function smooth boxes for storing your meals. To meal prep efficiently, take out all the meals objects you may want in advance than you begin cooking. Have your recipe to hand and installation the meals devices inside the order you may use them. Start strolling with the meals devices that take the longest time (normally cutting the end stop end result and greens). If you have become equipped raw meat, fish, chicken or unique animal products, make certain to apply a separate lowering board. Cross-infection can take place, specifically in case you are lowering salad or extremely good meals objects as a way to be eaten uncooked. For easier meal prep, make sure you have got proper system for the activity. For instance, get a exceptional knife and reducing boards and declutter your kitchen so that you have enough space.

After the meal prep, it is important to settle down the meals as speedy as viable if you are not eating it right away. Reducing the temperature of the food from 60°C to ten°C internal hours eliminates the risk of bacterial boom. Hot meals must now not be packed or included with a lid. When the meals is cold sufficient, located a lid on it or percentage it in air-tight containers and positioned it inside the refrigerator(sixty 3). The fridge temperature is suggested to be beneath 7°C in maximum worldwide locations, whilst below 5°C in a few, so make certain that your refrigerator is bloodless sufficient(sixty four). Put the dishes that want to keep the lowest temperature at the lowest of the fridge for the super sturdiness. Most meals maintain nicely inside the refrigerator for two to 3 days. If you make more food than you could consume in advance than it spoils, make certain to location it in the freezer proper away after the cooldown. When reheating cold food, ensure you warmness it as an lousy lot as approximately 70°C, as maximum bacteria will no longer live on this temperature(sixty 5). Below is a desk illustrating durability ranges for particular types of dishes, but continuously use your senses while evaluating the food(sixty six).

Hygiene – smooth fingers, tool, and tables

Strategize your meal prep

Have properly gadget

Be privy to the sturdiness of the meals that is prepped

Table 11. This table indicates great kinds of dishes and meals gadgets and their durability stored in carton, bag or bowl in the fridge. Remember that the fridge temperature, hygiene even as making ready the meals, and the field will play a factor in figuring out the durability of the meals.

NUTRITION "ON THE GO"

When you travelling locally, as an instance, to art work or brilliant sports activities sports, it's remarkable to have prepared meals that you can consume. The food you're making your self might be more healthy than food at meals stores(67). However, every so often it is hard to maintain food round. You would possibly probable have forgotten it at domestic or possibly eaten the whole lot already. In this scenario, it's miles treasured to apprehend what styles of meals items may be beneficial to buy as a snack.

These elements can be based at the thoughts noted in advance, with sluggish-digesting (fiber-rich) carbohydrates, some quality protein, and healthful fat. If the food gadgets have those components, it manner that they will be nutrient-dense as nicely (i.E., contain numerous micronutrients). If you've got were given have been given the time to prep some smooth-to-consume snacks, this might be hundreds less high priced than comparable options you should purchase. However, in case you do not have time to prepare any snacks, which products might be possible as a snack?

PRE-PACKED ON-THE-GO SNACKS

If you tour masses, purchase ice packs and a cooler. This manner you can prepare a number of proper meals earlier than you leave domestic to revel in for your travels.

There are many examples of tasty snack food. Some are stated earlier in the each day meal plan examples. The table underneath offers you a few extra examples of snacks you can make your self. The critical aspect is that those food need to be saved appropriately in order that they do no longer smash. For instance, if you make a sandwich, located it in a zip-lock bag or a lunch field. If you use dinner left-overs and can not preserve the food saved in a refrigerator, you should buy lunch bins with ice packs built in. Otherwise, you should buy ice packs and placed them next to your lunch box in a bag. Other meals devices that can art work splendid as a snack however need to be stored cold are cottage cheese, yogurt, smoothies, and quark. Nuts and give up end result with peel are not a trouble. They can tolerate each warmth and bloodless and, to some extent, excursion, and they'll be clean to eat. A handful of nuts in a zip-lock bag could now not take lots area, either, and can be carried for your pocket.

Table 12. The table shows examples of diverse snacks you can make yourself. These examples are meant for inspirational functions.

BOUGHT SNACKS

If you haven't organized any snacks, there are, of path, feasible alternatives to buy, especially if you have the information and time to examine the meals labels. As a modern day rule of thumb for snack meals, my advice could be snacks low on brought sugar and trans- and saturated fat. Food objects with some of sugar commonly do no longer consist of a number of nutrients, and that they spike the blood sugar unnecessarily. That technique gadgets like candy, doughnuts, ice cream, power liquids and sodas with sugar, chocolate, and masses of energy bars. You might imagine that isn't uncommon experience, however at the equal time as you're hungry and tempted by using manner of these meals gadgets, even the most effective energy of will may succumb. Avoiding snack food with a excessive content material cloth of volatile fats is likewise important, for lots precise health reasons. This manner foods like burgers, pizzas, and hot-puppies. They consist of many extra calories than a regular snack meal and normally offer a ways much much less version in nutrients and minerals. So, what must you buy? Well, the examples referred to above in the pre-packed snack segment may additionally offer belief. However, you could moreover purchase wholemeal sandwiches and baguettes with chook, ham, and cheese or eggs. Sometimes you could additionally find shops selling small dinner quantities. However, maximum of those examples are very luxurious in comparison to what you can make your self.

Chapter 6: Tournament Preparations

This phase will cover advice for fit settings, from earlier than excursion up until occasion end. Depending on in which and the way lengthy you can compete, making plans and packing certain food gadgets can be an crucial element for a pressure-free journey. The course and the space you journey will decide the effect to your health. Jetlag (circadian desynchronization), tour fatigue, and hygiene are commonplace demanding situations for athletes who tour hundreds.

BEFORE YOU TRAVEL

Depending on how a long way and lengthy you tour, making plans what to take with you can be important for fitness and performance. If you get sick or are not properly acclimatized, your overall performance can suffer. Usually, a number of information is to be had earlier than you excursion: in which the occasion is taking vicinity, what the accommodations may be like, and the period of the event. Jetlag can occur, and in the ones situations, the tour itinerary should be carefully planned. Travelling may be taxing, mainly if the journey time is extended. Meal styles get changed, you get uncovered to a amazing surroundings, pressure ranges would possibly increase, and training physical games is probably adjusted.

If you're familiar with touring, it is easy to estimate the kind and quantity of meals and water you'll need. Bottled water is usually to be had in maximum hotels. However, the terrific of the meals isn't always so dependable. For lengthy trips, it's far important now not to be dependent on buying meals all the time. Make sure you p.C. A lunchbox before you go away home, in addition to a few snacks you could devour if no specific meals is to be had. Depending at the length of your enjoy, your lunch box should include dinner left-overs (if the lunchbox has ice packs or if the meals is eaten speedy after being packed), sandwiches, crispbreads or baguettes. Finger components together with sandwiches are clean to eat. Good examples of snack meals are nuts, dried fruit or give up result with a peel. Protein bars can be beneficial, regardless of the reality that a whole lot of those bars are complete of sugars and occasional on micronutrients. As with every dried fruits and nuts, bars normally have great sturdiness. They are commonly packed in plastic which permits you to consume with out touching the meals without delay. Bars also can tolerate a few versions in temperature.

WHILE TRAVELING

While traveling, it's miles vital to be aware about your hydration. Changes in bowel conduct are frequent at the same time as touring, in part due to dehydration, but moreover due to a lack of motion and the extent of food intake(sixty eight). Make excellent you drink sufficient, however there's no need to overhydrate. Try to preserve a normal ingesting sample if you typically are hydrated. Buy bottled water while travelling. If you've got problems with constipation, attention on fiber-wealthy components on the aspect of prunes and kiwifruit. Be aware that after touring to remote places with extra than a five-hour time difference, the superiority of contamination will growth - to three-fold(sixty nine; 70). Being round an entire lot of human beings, in a modern-day environment with a special climate and new pathogens can growth the danger of turning into sick. Personal hygiene is vital. Wash your hands often and continuously earlier than you consume. Try to preserve your hands some distance out of your face. Carry with you hand sanitizers, even though they do no longer shield in addition to an remarkable hand wash. While journeying, search for meals which include end result with a peel, bags of nuts and dried fruit, pre-packed sandwiches, or special food that are clean to devour at the skip.

JETLAG

Jetlag takes location because of a mismatch the diverse circadian rhythms and the outdoor 24-hour mild-dark cycle; it usually happens after trans-meridian adventure through severa time zones. The effect can get stronger the more time zones are crossed. Also, the path of journey has an impact(seventy one). The signs of jetlag are fatigue, disturbed sleep, insomnia, decreased alertness, mood disturbance, belly troubles, temper modifications, decreased motivation, and hypersomnia(sixty eight). Obviously, numerous of these symptoms may be negative to an esports athlete's performance. Zeitgebers are rhythmic cues in the surrounding environment that assist align the internal body clock to this out of doors environment(seventy one). Apart from mild, this is the most effective zeitgeber, there are indicators that a few nutritional strategies may additionally help in alleviating the outcomes of jetlag. Supplementation with melatonin or caffeine and manipulation of meal timing and composition are used on this regard.

MELATONIN

Melatonin is synthesized from serotonin in the pineal gland. Sleep usually starts offevolved offevolved whilst there may be a concomitant upward thrust in melatonin and a fall in frame temperature(71). The effectiveness of melatonin supplementation may be very depending at the timing of administration, with a segment give a boost to in circadian rhythm happening at the same time as supplemented in the afternoon or night and a segment remove at the same time as taken in the early morning(68). Most research at the effect of melatonin supplementation on jetlag consists of dosages from two to eight mg with eastward tour wherein section amplify is wanted. Most of the research have established improved sleep and plenty less signs and symptoms of jetlag at a few level in the day(seventy one). However, be aware of capacity side consequences at the aspect of bewilderment, complications, hypnotic consequences and allergic reactions(seventy two). Countries have different tips concerning the availability of melatonin, so relying on in which you stay, it is probably difficult to purchase melatonin. In a few states, it is taken into consideration medication. Melatonin is available in notable office work, inclusive of liquids, drugs, and tablets, and might contain herbs or weight loss program and mineral combinations. Be aware that the melatonin content material can also have large variations however the labeling, with a batch-to-batch variability of up to 465%(seventy three). With such mixed nutritional dietary supplements, there may be furthermore the capacity risk of ingesting banned materials.

CAFFEINE

Caffeine is one of the most typically used approach of reducing daylight hours fatigue because of jetlag. Several research have counseled a great advantage of caffeine with jetlag or shift-art work sickness, which encompass advanced reasoning, decreased sleepiness, and a more speedy resynchronization fee. The protocols commonly utilized in those research are two hundred mg and 300 mg, that are quite huge dosages, relying on frame weight(68). This amount of caffeine can be determined in to 4 cups of coffee, relying on the type of coffee(74). Be aware that caffeine in big dosages can yield detail consequences which is probably terrible for health and gaming overall performance(1).

MEAL TIMING AND COMPOSITION

Less research has been completed on meal timing and composition on the subject of jetlag; as a result robust hints aren't made(sixty eight). However, I even have mentioned the capability mechanisms and food devices which would probable assist result in sleep. Food items wealthy in tryptophan, e.G., dairy products, might be actually worth which incorporates within the pre-sleep meal to probably enhance sleep wonderful. Also, going to bed hungry might be destructive to sleep notable(1). Manipulation of macronutrient composition may also be a method; however, more studies is wanted.

AT THE EVENT

When accommodated, make certain to plan food consistent with the event and different sports. There are often delays due to technical issues, so make sure to percentage a few easy-to-devour snacks on workout day. Fruits with a peel, nuts, dried end result, protein bars, and sandwiches are pinnacle alternatives when you have little spare time to eat. If you are out sightseeing the various fits, it can be smart to avoid close by road food due to lack of awareness about hygiene practices. Instead, use neighborhood human beings for advice on correct ingesting locations. If you are ingesting from the buffet, look for freshly prepared dishes and avoid meals that seems like it is been there for some time. Note how the meals is furnished inside the buffet area; heat meals need to be particularly heat, no longer lukewarm. If it is cold meals, ensure it's far at fridge temperature and no longer warmth. In preferred, try to avoid raw eggs, undercooked and raw meat, shellfish and seafood, unpasteurized dairy merchandise, raw salads and veggies, and fruit that cannot be peeled. This relies upon on in that you're travelling, with a few locations having a higher risk than others of meals contamination. Finally, in case you are staying in a house, purchase meals from the local grocery shops so you do no longer must eat out all the time. It each saves cash and makes it easier to carry snacks to the occasion. If you are staying in a motel, use the mini-bar to your room to preserve snacks that need to be saved bloodless.

DURING THE GAMES

There is generally little time to consume something even as playing, due to the individual of the game. Usually, there are some seconds among every spherical, wherein gamers commonly rehydrate. In most instances, the brilliant component to carry is a water bottle. Keeping yourself hydrated is vital for famous cognitive overall overall performance. If, however, you're playing for extended intervals of time, and you haven't any meals to be had or urge for meals to devour some detail, a sports drink can be used. Sports liquids generally encompass sugars (e.G., glucose, fructose, maltodextrin), electrolytes, vitamins, and/or minerals. Some sports sports liquids additionally include caffeine. However, be aware that lots of sugar will have an effect to your blood sugar stage and shouldn't be used with out an first-rate approach. One example wherein sports activities sports beverages or comparable products is probably used beneficially is while gambling in a opposition for a prolonged period of time.

An instance of this is a great-of-5 in DOTA2 (Defense of the Ancients 2). The excellent-of-five can take many hours, relying on the results. Ingesting those liquids is probably some element to consider during the last couple of video video games. The exquisite possibility, however, is to devour some awesome food. It does not want to be some thing fancy, and it have to no longer be masses of food. Usually, there can be some-mins wreck between fits. In this spoil, there may be an possibility to eat some thing. Examples of meals that doesn't have an impact on the blood sugar an excessive amount of, whilst giving some correct power and experience of fullness, are wholemeal sandwiches or crispbreads and fruits with a peel. Try now not to overeat inside the route of these snack food, as this will be counterproductive due to the effect large food (especially those wealthy in carbohydrates) have on blood sugar levels.

Chapter 7: Newest Billion-Dollar Industry

We're all gamers. You, your grandma, and your little cousin In fact, pretty plenty all and sundry you recognize is a gamer. People of every age and backgrounds play a few sort of cellular, console, or PC task You're (in all likelihood) a gamer. Otherwise, why are you reading this ebook? For you, it might be the most present day launch on a modern console. Or possibly you built your very very own PC. You may additionally additionally also be into VR.

Your grandma? You higher recollect she's dabbled a hint in Solitaire or Candy Crush on Facebook.

Your little cousin? He's probable "cranking ninety's" on Fortnite.

As we said on the start of this e-book, the gaming enterprise is blowing up. Games have worked their manner into pretty much every era and manner of existence.

And, as gaming keeps to develop, so is gaming-associated content material material on-line and esports. The greater people sport themselves, the greater they choose to examine unique people gaming. Why? Because it's far a way to keep considering the video games you adore even on the same time as you are not gambling yourself.

Esports has blown up for a few special reason, too. The way we eat media has modified. Traditional TV, which capabilities conventional sports activities and content material, has been modified with YouTube, Twitch, and social media.

The largest celebrities in recent times aren't movie or TV stars. They're YouTubers and streamers. They're social media influencers. People's attention is shifting to a part of the internet in which gaming content material fabric is already sturdy.

Football and basketball may additionally dominate the cable channels, but gaming and esports already have a foothold inside the new, cellular model of TV.

When interest shifts from TV to content cloth cloth creators, the coins is brief to check, as nicely. Just a couple of years in the past, businesses likely idea a sponsorship or emblem address an influencer or content creator turn out to be a "volatile flow into." At that point, TV classified ads and conventional sports activities sports sponsorships felt more stable, attempted and right. But, nowadays, increasingly more manufacturers are catching on. They see wherein human beings's eyes and minds are, and so the cash and advertising and marketing and advertising and marketing and advertising is shifting over to esports, content material creators, and social media influencers.

Just how big is esports and gaming in comparison to conventional sports sports? We'll solution that question on this financial disaster. But first, permit's take a glance once more on the origins of esports.

Where did the today's billion-greenback enterprise come from? How has it grown over the years? And what can we see approximately its destiny?

Let's answer the ones questions now.

A Crash Course in Esports History

Esports is older than you observed. In truth, you could see online game tournaments relationship as some distance back because of the reality the 1970's. Remember in the antique days even as people could probable visit arcades to play big cabinet games, like Mrs. Pacman and Donkey Kong? Each hobby had a excessive rating, and youngsters may additionally play coin after coin for a risk to conquer the current excessive rating. Local tournaments ensued, drawing hundreds of hobby for the arcade proprietors.

In 1972, what many go through in mind the number one first rate gaming competition befell at Stanford University. Players competed to get the very nice rating in a sport referred to as Spacewar.

Years later, even as the Atari come to be all the rage, tournaments began out up all over again. In 1980, as an example, the Atari Space Invaders Championship attracted 10,000 gamers.

Later, we see Nintendo hit the scene. The Nintendo World Championships in 1990 toured the usa of a, collecting up the extremely good gamers for a completely ultimate showdown at Universal Studios in California. A second Nintendo Championship grow to be held in 1994 to sell the Super NES console device.

By the overdue 90's we started out out seeing the number one esport leagues, with names together with Cyberathlete Professional League (CPL), the Professional Gamers League, and Quakecon. As that final name shows, a number one recreation utilized in competitions at the time modified into Quake, notwithstanding the truth that Counter-Strike and Warcraft had been large for esports, too.

Early gaming competitions and tournaments had a few similarities to fashionable esports, but the game hadn't simply superior but. In 1997, the primary esports competition that felt like a current occasion have become held, focusing on the sport Quake.

This match was known as The Red Annihilation. Over 2,000 humans competed on-line, preventing every one-of-a-kind in 1v1 Quake suits. When the player pool modified into whittled right all the way down to 16 gamers, those 16 were flown to Atlanta, Georgia to compete live!

eSports endured to grow from there. The Worldwide Webgames Championship changed into held in 2006, organized with the useful resource of FUN Technologies. Seventy-one players competed for a million-dollar prize.

Nintendo once more to the esports scene in 2010 with the Wii Games. This is whilst Super Smash Brothers have been given its start as a primary esports call.

Of course, in 2011, the entirety changed with the appearance of Twitch. For the number one time, a platform existed that (almost) completely shows gaming content material material fabric. Early Twitch streamers had been given well-known with the aid of manner of gambling pretty aggressive games like League of Legends and Dota 2.

For the primary time, the ones esports titles have been additionally spectator sports, with tens of hundreds of lots of humans searching others play and compete.

While esports has never been all that large on TV in the U.S., at least in no way in comparison to online viewerships, places like Twitch made it possible for hundreds of thousands of fans to revel in looking others play their preferred games. Esports continued to develop after that into what it's miles in recent times.

The World of Esports and Streaming Now

As we said on the outset of this financial catastrophe, every body is a gamer nowadays, and the gaming fashion is ready to hold growing over the subsequent couple of years. What does this recommend for esports and streaming? Let's crunch some numbers to find out.

Let's start via searching at the increase of gaming itself, breaking things down through age agency.

Gamers--Young and Old

One effective way to peer that gaming is at the upward push is to peer that extra more youthful audiences are into gaming more than ever.

"But wait," you may say. "Of course youngsters play video video video games extra. They're kids!"

Well, we each recognize that the gaming organisation is entire of titles for each more younger and mature game enthusiasts. The problem of having older dad and mom into gaming is that you need to introduce them to a concept that wasn't spherical once they had been youngsters. But topics are changing, one year with the aid of the usage of one year, because we've got were given kids nowadays that have had a mobile phone or iPad of their possession for as long as they could take into account. Heck, a few kids in recent times are gambling a few type of cellular sport earlier than they're able to even communicate!

As those kids become older, they will not prevent gaming. They'll without a doubt pick out up an increasing number of complex and mature video video games to spend their money and time on.

This manner that, as generations develop antique, gaming, streaming, and esports will preserve growing.

But, as I said earlier, permit's check some numbers.

According to Newzoo, about 80% of Gen Z and Millennials play a few form of virtual endeavor.

This is large for every streaming and esports, as we're capable of see underneath, as it method every sponsors and advertisers may be looking for to spend their greenbacks with the gaming enterprise as it maintains to growth.

The commonplace Baby Boomer gamers-- antique humans, probably your grandparents--play a median of 6 hours and 50 mins consistent with week. Nearly half of humans your grandparents' age admit to gaming at least an hour each week.

Of direction, the more youthful you move within the ballot Newzoo positioned out, the extra gamers you discover. Sixty percent of Gen Xer's are gamers, seventy seven% of millennials, and 80 one% of Gen Zer's. Gen Zer's spend a mean of 7 hours and 20 minutes every week gambling video video video games!

PC vs Console vs Mobile

Of route, PC and console gaming are not going anywhere. You can be a diehard PC recreation fan, or you may pick to interest with a PlayStation or Xbox controller for your hand. Those regions of the gaming global are on the upward push and will live strong for a very long term.

That said, it is clean that gaming is slowly shifting to cellular.

Newzoo's poll suggests that, in every era they wondered, mobile gaming is the pinnacle platform for everybody.

That stated, greater younger generations appear to like gaming on any platform. While seventy seven% of Gen Zer's say they interest on cellular, sixty eight% moreover say that they play at the PC and fifty 8% moreover say they play on console. Put the ones possibilities together and it is clean--a large sort of kids in recent times are platform agnostic. In truth, cross-platform video video games (together with the appearance of cloud gaming) are on the rise. Millennials had very similar numbers, by using the way.

So what's the route of video video games as far as platform? All systems are at the upward push. Mobile, of course, is developing faster. This is in part because it's the most much less high priced alternative. You can purchase a pair-hundred-dollar cellphone or tablet and, the usage of some cloud gaming subscription choice like Google Stadia or

Apple Arcade, you may play all styles of immoderate-give up video games--so long as you've got a quick sufficient internet connection.

While lots of human beings even though assemble their non-public gaming PCs, or in reality purchase the shockingly suitable gaming laptops and consoles to be had in recent times, some of humans do not problem. They just live with the choice it's of their pocket all the time except--cellular!

What This Means for Streaming

So gaming--and an hobby in video video games--is at the rise. And gaming is turning into increasingly platform-agnostic with a slight leaning toward cellular and cloud gaming. What does all of this mean for the streaming agency?

As you can probably wager, streaming is surely on the upward push!

Of more youthful game enthusiasts polled by means of the usage of Newzoo, seventy one% additionally watch gaming content. The pinnacle content material kind is gameplay content cloth, (let's performs and assignment tutorials) with a near 2nd being comedic gaming motion images and compilations.

Basically, the extra people play video games themselves, they reflect onconsideration on video video games and need to examine one-of-a-kind humans play them, too. And, as content material material intake starts offevolved to lean an increasing number of inside the course of mobile, gamers are selecting their favorite streamer or gaming content fabric creator over Netflix or Disney Plus.

According to Juniper Research, recreation streaming goes to upward push extra than 70% over the subsequent four years.

And, of course, as extra people spend time looking streamers and gaming content fabric fabric creators, increasingly agencies will take gain by means of using sponsoring or marketing and advertising. By 2025, one projection says the streaming agency is probably making over $3.Five billion!

Don't you want a bit of that pie? Even the thinnest of slices would be greater than sufficient to update a complete-time hobby.

What This Means for Esports

Streaming isn't the pleasant thing of gaming way of life that has exploded in latest years. Esports is also on the rise. As we stated within the introduction of this e-book, esports is projected to end up one thousand million-dollar industry in 2021.

In truth, via a few projections, esports will keep growing at least 14% each 365 days for the following severa years.

Once again, as esports grows in recognition and viewership, so will sponsorship and advertising and marketing and advertising and advertising and marketing cash spent on esports.

Last 12 months, there were an anticipated 90 million esports web site site visitors. Even as esports took a fulfillment because of the pandemic no longer permitting massive in-individual tournaments to expose up, due to the fact an hobby in gaming continued to expand global-enormous, viewership in fact recovered, and keeps to broaden, in 2021.

Mature markets for esports, together with in North America and Western Europe, maintain growing, but secondary markets, which embody the Middle East, Africa,

Asia-Pacific, and Latin America are experiencing even more increase.

Because gaming, streaming, and esports are all viable on cell these days, cellular-first markets, which incorporates India and Brazil, are exploding in viewership inside the last couple of years and will maintain to accomplish that.

As esports grows in popularity, so does esports recognition. What does that endorse?

Think approximately it this manner: Even if you do now not play American Football, or even watch a single pastime all yr, approximately the game. You probable recognize the names of some top gamers and teams, and you could even recognise approximately whilst the Super Bowl is, too. Why? Because American Football is vital to American manner of life... at the least for max households.

As esports will become more well-known, even people that have no hobby in gaming are being attentive to approximately it. That manner esports are also becoming extra well-known as a legitimate shape of pastime.

This is critical for the boom of income in esports because the CEO's and advertising and advertising and advertising and marketing corporations for producers, the human beings that determine in which to spend advertising and advertising and advertising and marketing and sponsorship coins, are inclined to entertain the concept of spending a number of that money in esports, despite the fact that those enterprise company parents do no longer sport themselves in any respect.

Chapter 8: Three Tips to Build Your Foundation

The direction to turning into a top participant inside the global of gaming is not through mountaineering a company ladder or getting a organization degree. No, the direction is in developing content material fabric material, streaming, building an target market and emblem, and making connections with different people in the agency.

In this economic catastrophe, I'm going to reveal you the way to get started out with a career in gaming.

This direction isn't always a concrete blueprint. It isn't one-duration-suits-all. Instead, similar to an open-world pastime, that is a pick your private journey.

Instead of sharing a tough and fast of steps, I'm going to percent 3 guiding requirements, 3 of my fantastic Insider

Tips for helping you get started out with a career in gaming and esports.

So, with out further ado, allow's start with my first tip.

Insider Tip #1: Get Immersed In Gaming Communities

You're analyzing this book due to the fact you're a gamer. You love playing your favourite titles, whether or not those are first-character shooters, MMORPGs, or 4x or method games. You are in all likelihood already plugged into some gaming communities at some level.

Do you ever touch upon the Youtube video of your selected gaming content material fabric writer? Are you a part of Facebook corporations that middle around your chosen gaming titles or game genre? Do you ever chat alongside facet your pals approximately video video games on

Discord? If so, you then're already a part of a growing on line gaming network.

So my first tip for you is to get more lively, to gain out and get immersed in as many elements of that community as you in all likelihood can.

Look for boards, channels on discord, and gaming subreddits. The greater worried you turn out to be, the more the advantages. Speaking of benefits, what are you able to preference to benefit from diving even deeper into severa gaming companies? Below are four particular buffs you can assume from network immersion.

Community Benefit #1: You'll Love Gaming--and Specific Games More--via using Connecting With Others Who Share Your Passion

Have you ever discovered that your love of a particular pastime comes and is going at times? Perhaps you are hooked on a certain name for days, weeks, or maybe months, and then your passion wanes. Then, later, you rediscover how a laugh and tough the perceive is, and you marvel why you gave up gambling it inside the first place!

Some titles, like the ones inside the distinctly well-known battle royale style, can begin to experience pretty repetitive after a while. Other video games, like MMORPGs, among others, encourage you to grind for limitless hours on the equal maps, performing the identical obligations over and over.

Playing the ones kinds of games in isolation can get boring. But being a part of a passionate community for such video games unlocks a whole new diploma of gameplay. The social element is the maximum exciting part of many video video games, and game enthusiasts will often create their non-public annoying conditions, alliances, and achievements that make the sport a whole lot extra a laugh for limitless hundreds of hours of greater gameplay.

Another fun length of many video games lies in the modding community. Community individuals add mods, skins, and network-powered maps, and each of these additions can upload a smooth address a acquainted name.

Community Benefit #2: You Improve Your Games Through Forums, Tutorials, and Let's Plays

Another fundamental gain of getting truely immersed in gaming communities has to do at the side of your talents diploma inside the games you play.

We've all probably had that one sport as kids that we cherished and finished for hours on stop... Till we had been given to that one diploma that certainly stumped us. As difficult as we tried, we might also want to in no way get beyond it. As a result, our hobby in the game waned, and we moved on to one in all a kind subjects.

Of course, nowadays, that may be a minor trouble that new generations of game enthusiasts don't need to worry about. Why?

Because YouTube is full of awesome walkthrough and educational films--and network boards and subreddits are complete of hints, tricks, and step-with the useful aid of-step tutorials, as nicely--you can in no manner get caught in a sport again.

And, connecting once more to the preceding advantage, as you improve your skills in a game, the extra passionate you are probable to be about that call. On pinnacle of that, as you decorate to your skills, the greater clout you will advantage in organizations that cost pinnacle gamers of that unique sport. When you start developing content and streaming, as we are going to speak approximately within the following bankruptcy, you will be higher able to trap a huge following the higher you're at a activity.

Community Benefit #three: Online Communities Help Get You More In Tune With The Gaming Industry--Both The Industry At Large and Specific Segments Within It.

In my 2nd Insider Tip (arising), I talk approximately making yourself beneficial to severa components of the esports and gaming employer. You'll most effective be capable of do this in case you apprehend what's taking vicinity in the international of gaming.

Sure, you can take a look at up on gaming records by means of way of subscribing to 3 warm blogs, which include esports.Gg and Dexerto, and you may observe plenty about what is happening inside the international of gaming from searching streamers and checking Twitter for esports healthy insurance and breaking gaming data, however there's no longer whatever better than entering into the middle of it, paying attention to the news because it's occurring in real-time, and mastering the movers and shakers in a selected location of the organisation.

Game developers and esports officers frequent many well-known gaming network forums, and maximum have lively and insightful Twitter bills. Through those channels, they share dispositions and mind with individuals of these companies in advance than anyone else is aware of about them.

The greater time you spend in that particular place, the greater you may experience in music with wherein gaming and esports are going inside the months and future years. That will help you begin questioning in very sensible phrases concerning profession opportunities within the global of gaming.

Community Benefit #4: Finally, Getting Involved In Online Gaming Communities Helps You To Build and Grow A Network In The Industry.

You recognize the antique adage: "It's no longer what you already know, it is who you understand," right? Well, it is truely actual inside the worldwide of esports and gaming.

Think about the example noted on the start of this bankruptcy. Dr Disrespect became searching out a key function in his newly-forming endeavor dev studio.

Where did he flip to look for the proper humans to characteristic to his organization? LinkedIn? Indeed.Com? Upwork? No, he grew to emerge as to his huge target market. Within hours of his real tweet over 17,000 people had preferred and retweeted the message. That name for some very particular humans to fill some very precise job positions unfold through an intensive community of--you guessed it--gamers!

Now, in that example, Dr Disrespect had a massive following to achieve out to, however many esports companies and smaller indie pastime developers do the same every day. They benefit out to the human beings they have related with on line after they want someone to enroll in their crew.

Building and developing a network thru the gaming network is a want to in case you need to recognize approximately possibilities or get discovered. Even in case you sense you're years away from substantially trying to find a career in gaming, you can begin now with the resource of organically growing a community thru using connecting with all the right channels on Twitter, using Twitch Chats, and constructing connections thru boards and community message forums and corporations. Of path, even in this excellent-on-line global, probable the amazing way to network is in man or woman, thru gaming conventions and community meet-ups.

Bonus Benefit: You Can Start to Establish Your Audience

As we already said, the following bankruptcy will popularity clearly on streaming and why you want to start developing content material cloth as rapid as feasible if you need to get observed in the global of gaming. When you do start developing content fabric fabric, who do you determined your first actual subscribers and followers may be? Why, people you have related with in diverse businesses, of route!

As you community and make buddies on Twitter, Youtube, and Twitch, you will be planting the seeds for a beginning target audience for your future streaming ventures.

So there you have got it: Four benefits of getting immersed in on-line gaming communities. Plus an advantage!

But, earlier than we skip onto my 2d Insider Tip, I need to deal with an vital precept that all of us need to have a examine even as wearing out online gaming groups.

Be Respectful of Others

This is an apparent one. Like we said above, all network pointers consist of regulations that essentially boil right right down to "do not be a jerk." But this hassle is very critical.

No recall what you are speakme about, constantly be respectful of different gamers. Don't allow clearly every person drag you down into an ugly combat. Why now not? Because your document on-line is your resume. It's your brand as a streamer. Years from now, people can be able to pass lower lower back and tune down each tweet you made, every statement you made on any discussion board, and republish the ones matters in your future fans and employers to look.

Online celebrities all reduce to rubble from time to time, saying some factor they probable ought to no longer. Or from time to time subjects may be taken out of context later. You cannot assist all of that.

But if you attempt your high-quality to be respectful usually, you may stand out as a frontrunner in the organizations you commonplace.

Insider Tip #2: Engage and Interact

Let's say you have already began out following my first Insider Tip. You've come to be immersed in online gaming agencies and gaming news. You are definitely up to date with the gaming corporation and you are developing an in depth community of gaming friends. Awesome!

But now it's time to take that a step in addition. The cause of this 2d tip, at the side of Insider Tip #three, which we will communicate about underneath, is to take you from community member to community leader. In order to do that, you need to begin interacting with great leaders in the gaming enterprise.

How do you do this? By tweeting, messaging, and interacting with streamers, leaders, and companies that relate to the video video games you like to play.

And I apprehend from private experience that this works like a attraction. I simply have had a ton of achievement inside the past surely publicly tweeting at humans I even have 0 connection with. More instances than now not, I are becoming some shape of reaction. More than more than one times, that small interaction delivered about a cutting-edge door of possibility for me in the future.

The lesson? It in no manner hurts to shoot your shot!!!

Go Ahead! Be Annoying!

I realise what you'll be questioning proper now. "I do now not want to be demanding! Why have to I begin tweeting crucial businesses and gaming celebrities?"

But I'm going to inform you the fact approximately being stressful: there's no such issue.

In fact, even as you placed up your hand and engage with leaders and public figures in your favored nook of the gaming enterprise, you're displaying you care. You're putting yourself aside.

Comment and Engage

Think of it this manner: Go to a gaming-themed video on YouTube, a totally well-known one. How many views are there at the video?

Now test how many feedback were on that equal video. Do a piece math. Divide the style of views by using the variety of comments.

By doing this you will find that loads of people ought to view a video for every observation.

So even as you make an effort to comment on each video you watch, you are mechanically putting yourself above hundreds or maybe loads of human beings that do not even hassle to statement in any respect.

Now what in case you take some time to write down a thoughtful commentary for each video. What if those comments get found via exclusive visitors and even the streamer that located out the video inside the first area? Can you note in which that might lead you?

Again, I apprehend this works from non-public revel in. I have acquired new lovers due to the truth humans have positioned my profile from a observation and determined that I myself grow to be a content material fabric material writer, so that they determined and started out searching my streams.

Before you apprehend it, you could see that leaders inside the gaming enterprise will do not forget you through call. That's due to the fact you've got established up time and again. You took the time to interact and engage at the same time as each person else simply passively watched the motion pix and moved at once to the subsequent one.

Try it on Twitter, Too

What in case you took the time to direct message and tweet business enterprise leaders publicly, as well? What's the worst that might take location?

Again, you will be questioning which you do not need to problem people. But hold in mind that public figures often collect thousands of messages every day. It is a extraordinary deal greater normal these days for people of have an effect directly to have conversations and respond to their fanatics on social media. Don't fear if you in no manner acquire a reaction. Even if they did no longer respond, it does not suggest that they have got not taken word! The seed has been planted.

I could now not have become half of the opportunities I've had in my profession if I hadn't reached out to humans publicly on Twitter. So I understand it genuinely works!

Sure, maximum of the human beings you message or tweet might not answer you. And it's appropriate sufficient! Major streamers or recreation developers are busy oldsters. And in reality because of the truth someone didn't reply, does now not mean that they have not taken phrase! The seed is planted!

Try this: Tweet a person publicly, however do no longer ask for a few thing. Don't even ask a query. Make excessive exceptional your tweet does not require any sort of response. Just commend a person for their tough artwork. Tell them you understand the content material they make or the sport they designed. Be actual about it.

And repeat this method frequently! Stay within the the the front of human beings's minds!

There is, of route, a nice line among messaging humans to commend them and asking for some element. Your primary purpose proper here is to be visible, not to beg for help or a handout. It's critical to continuously be within the kingdom of mind that you need to provide charge, in no manner requesting charge.

You may be amazed how often you may get a reaction from such remarks. And, even at the identical time as you don't, I promise you'll be located and remembered.

Chapter 9: How Streaming Can Become Your Full-Time Job

Live streaming has emerged as the most up to date growing detail of on line content fabric cloth advent. And as soon as I say "freshest growing," I suggest each with developing audiences and with growing hobby from entrepreneurs.

Let's take a second to look clearly how a ways streaming has come.

About a decade within the beyond, streamers have been the black sheep of the net content material-introduction own family. Youtubers were making it big, and the idea of being a social media influencer changed into clearly beginning to take off. But streaming a few sport you are playing? That wasn't absolutely a possible preference for turning into a profession opportunity. It grow to be some thing you just did for fun.

Of route, as a substitute, the era wasn't in reality there, but, either. Internet speeds and gaming PCs have been fast sufficient to way an A-tier game and first rate audio and video of the gamer. We did now not have cloud streaming services like we do these days.

On pinnacle of that, there was nearly no stress (or capability) to enhance production nice. Most streamers did now not even hassle with a webcam, and for audio they used their gaming headset.

That manner maximum streaming content material material at that factor concerned someone gaming and recording their display even as you heard them talking through a tiny mic. You also can want to even pay interest many streamers breathing among sentences, their breath hitting the headset's mic. (Headsets, via the manner, like those from Astro &

Sennheiser and Razer, have advanced substantially, as properly.)

Compare that with the level of fine we see with many streamers nowadays.

These days, even a gaming computer of less pricey nice can control maximum video video games and streaming. With cloud-based completely streaming software software solutions, you do not need to tax your device to run the sport and the waft.

Many streamers have intricate setups, entire with sound-handled rooms, epic lights, and studio-brilliant microphones. They flow into in HD with a face cam, images and filters, and (of path) the cutting-edge games.

Streamers growth popular on-virtual digicam personalities, whole with catchphrases, strolling jokes, or maybe situation remember song.

Because of packages like Adobe Character Animator, even streamers that do not need to show up on camera have live lively avatars that skip, chuckle and talk in the bottom nook of the show.

As the splendid of streaming has risen, how has this affected the capacity of creating streaming a full-time interest, complete with an entire-time paycheck? But first, why are we speaking a lot approximately streaming? What if you need to become a expert gamer? Or what in case you want to, like me, begin casting? Or in all likelihood you've got have been given your elements of hobby set on some different aspect of aggressive gaming or the gaming agency.

Chapter 10: The Art of Discoverability

Let's say you start streaming today for the number one time. You have a PC and webcam and a simple USB mic you obtain from Best Buy. You boot up your preferred exercise (In this financial disaster, we'll use Rocket League as an example.), open your Twitch account, and get prepared. You've spent a few hours playing together together together with your streaming software program of preference, perhaps StreamLabs, and you acquire it walking honestly right.

Finally, you begin the motion.

You get into the sport, playing in shape after healthy. You snort and tell jokes as you bypass. Your Dad facilitates Grandma Betty pull your glide up on her pill. She can't parent out the manner to kind in chat. It's all appropriate even though, she's there. You enjoy like a film big name!

After an hour or , you appear to test your viewer rely. Surely, you purchased at the least a handful, right? Maybe even a dozen? Not lousy for a number one-timer...

The variety you spot shocks you. One? Just one viewer? After a number of these hours of incredible content material? All of the unexpected Grandma's assist feels disrespectful.

Well, you decide, at least you've got one viewer. That's a begin, right?

You close off the go with the flow and turn off Rocket League. You revel in like a failure. This will in no way art work, you inform yourself.

You become binging some thing on Netflix. You don't even want to consider streaming yet again. Maybe you're surely not reduce out for it. All those big streamers must have a few component you don't, right? Might as nicely in reality surrender in advance than you're making a idiot of your self…

Woah! Stop that horrible questioning!

Let's take a 2d to talk approximately discoverability. Why is it so essential? How are you capable of "get placed" and make it big as a streamer? Let's talk approximately that!

Streaming is a Big Deal—and that's each Good News and Bad News

Online gaming content fabric cloth and streaming is a constantly growing a part of the internet. We've talked plenty about how video games have become part of definitely absolutely everyone's lifestyles, old and young, and the way esports and gaming content material are on the upward thrust in a large manner.

Every day, masses of new people determine—inclusive of you—to start streaming on Twitch or YouTube or Facebook or some place else. Go to Twitch at quite plenty any time of the day and you'll see hundreds of people streaming in pretty plenty any category conceivable.

The truth that streaming is one of these large deal—and getting large with the aid of the day—is every specific information and horrible news. Let's take a look at the terrible news first.

The Bad News: It's Hard to get Noticed on Twitch

It's actual. When you go to any elegance in Twitch the default list suggests you streamers with the very superb quantity of visitors first. That way in advance than all of us can discover you, they need to scroll via all of the pinnacle streamers that passed off to be on line right now.

This is clearly awful data for ultra-modern streamers because of the fact they don't have anyone searching out them, proper?

Well, there can be a silver lining, which we'll speak about next.

The Good News: Discoverability is in Your Hands!

It is honestly actual that the way many systems are designed, together with Twitch, it could seem almost impossible for modern-day streamers to get located. If you don't have any web page traffic, regardless of everything, then how are you speculated to get extra website online traffic? Sounds like a chook-and-egg sort of trouble.

But proper proper right here's the coolest data: your boom in your palms! It's up to you to get observed, develop an target market, and construct a emblem people will understand and flock to. Then, as you do develop, structures like Twitch will reward that momentum with the aid of showing you more prominently to browsing visitors.

"I pay attention you," you might be announcing, "however how precisely is that pinnacle news?"

Well, keep in mind it this way: If you're on a sailboat within the center of the ocean, you're simply at the mercy of the wind to get you transferring, right? In historic instances, sailors ought to get stuck within the center of the big sea, simply bobbing there, due to the fact they have been given stuck in a period of no wind. Sailors may try to maintain busy, repairing the supply and stuff, but ultimately it grow to be a equipped endeavor.

Now don't forget you're in that state of affairs and someone offers you multiple oars. Or, even higher, a chunk gas motor.

Suddenly you have the strength to do some thing. You're lower once more on pinnacle of things of your supply!

In a whole lot the identical manner, humans that take the thoughts-set of having to appearance beforehand to the god-like algorithms to bless them with favorable winds might also furthermore become looking ahead to all time for that enhance. When topics don't rise up the way they want—they don't get the views or feedback or likes they expected—they blame the platform itself. "Twitch doesn't like me so I don't get any advertising. The YouTube set of hints gods have cursed me!"

But, whilst you understand that you have a motor, that you could pressure your very personal discoverability, and that Twitch isn't a few divine being that you want will word you and bless you with tens of tens of millions of lovers, then you get to take control of your private destiny!

In this bankruptcy, we're going to have a have a take a look at 3 Discoverability Tips that assist you to power site visitors to your Twitch drift or YouTube channel. These pointers acquired't assure you thousands and loads of web page visitors overnight, but they will provide you with the energy to steer your very very personal deliver and slowly chug along in the direction of your desires.

Discoverability Tip #1: Analyze the Competition

Let's hold with the above example and say you're a diehard Rocket League streamer. You simply commenced, and you've almost no subscribers. But you apprehend what recreation you need to focus on: permit's say via and massive Rocket League with a piece of Apex Legends for a trade of pace. Those are your all-time desired video games, after all.

If you need to be a pinnacle streamer for those titles, you want to analyze the opposition. Watch awesome streamers for the ones video video games, and try and decide out what they're doing that you can emulate.

In fact, allow's get a chunk extra centered than that. I want you to choose your "Top 12". What does that endorse?

Pick Your Top 12

Look on the top 12 streamers for your game of preference. Spend time watching them. Browse thru their VODs. Look at their social media. Really look at them.

In fact, permit's get even greater detailed. It isn't sufficient to sincerely choose out out the pinnacle 12 streamers that best play Rocket League together with you. You additionally want to discover the pinnacle 12 streamers which is probably of the same type as you.

Remember even as we mentioned streamer type? We talked about The Entertainer, The Professional, and The Tutor as three examples. So, which do you cause to be?

Let's say, for example, which you want to usually be an entertainer. You like making jokes as you play. You've continuously been right at making stupid voices and you can think rapid at the same time as gambling. You're referred to as a witty character.

Chapter 11: Competitive Play and Joining Teams

Going from gaming enthusiasm to professionalism takes time and willpower to the medium. It is in no way not feasible even though. If you play your playing cards cautiously, and take a look at your chosen mission indoors and out, you'll find out the complete device a excellent deal simpler than it in any other case may be. Remember that practice makes perfect, and that you gained't grow to be a seasoned in a single day.

Basic Tips to Give You the Edge in Popular eSports

League of Legends

League of Legends is one of the most popular and maximum earning eSports on the scene right now. A MOBA via using nature, it does have something of a steep analyzing curve. However, once you get the hold of factors, this enterprise turns into one in every of your go to options for a aggressive revel in.

When truely starting out, it's quite encouraged that you play in the route of the AI earlier than other players. Doing so permits you to get the draw near of the sport mechanics and guidelines, along element the danger to try multiple one-of-a-kind champions to see which play fashion fits you the top notch. During your not unusual game of League, there are numerous roles that you may play counting on the land which you pick out to attention on:

Top: These characters are your melee focused tanks. They attention on the top lane, because the call implies, and can and will deal and accumulate a whole lot of damage at some point of the route of the game. This lane isn't suitable to ranged or mana primarily based completely champions.

Mid: Focusing on the center lane, the ones champions usually play thru manner of themselves. Make sure that the champion you pick can deal and take heavy quantities of damage, and which you're organized to probable take out more than one champions right now.

Bot: Two gamers are traditionally assigned to the bottom lane: The ADC (Attack, Damage, Carry), and the assist. The ADC traditionally farms minions within the early to mid endeavor, and is a strain to be reckoned with by using the mid to late undertaking. Ranged champions, together with Ashe, are great for this feature as they could harass enemies with damage dealing number one attacks and devastating particular attacks.

The help historically is there to help the ADC. The number one dreams of these champions are to shield the ADC and to help in killing enemy champions.

Jungle: Jungle champions do now not have any specific assigned function inner League. Rather, they focus on killing the AI enemies in the "jungle", and helping distinct gamers when referred to as upon. Gnar is a exceptional example of a jungling champion. However, jungling is satisfactory averted till level twenty because of the volume of optimization that it has a tendency to require.

After experiencing multiple particular champions and play styles, begin focusing on individual optimization. During the sport, pay attention to the devices that end up available to you in the store. Purchase your gadgets based totally on the champion and the position which you're playing. For instance, an ADC individual at the facet of Ashe will need a excessive movement and assault velocity, more melee based honestly characters will need to consciousness on dealing better stages of damage at a faster price from their essential attacks, and ranged, mana based totally absolutely characters will want to interest on mana manufacturing and cool down discount. Character optimization is kind of infinitely variable based to your personal play style, and what the scenario at some point of the healthy calls for. If you may, try to provide your self a elegant idea of ways you need to optimize your character preceding to starting a new healthy.

Mastery factors and runes useful aid in character optimization outside of the primary sport. These buffs add to your assault harm, person speed, and other stats. If you've decided a play style that you like, it's truly well worth it to start constructing your rune tree and allocate your mastery factors as early as it will become possible in case you need to attain this. You can handiest have one net internet web page of masteries for all of your champions, so it's important to determine early on which stat wooden you'll select to max out.

While gambling the sport, especially if you're a amateur, do your remarkable to stay within the back of your minions and out of form of the towers you'll be attacking. Take more care to live out of the variety of more effective champions than yourself, till you're with any other player and feel confident to take them down. If you die a couple of instances thru the equal champion, it will become step by step greater hard to defeat them as the sport is going on. Death can come very speedy at a few level within the path of an come upon with an enemy champion, so watch out and don't be afraid to retreat in your organizations hub (using the B key) in case your champion is close to lack of lifestyles. The inverse, however, is also genuine. If you discover your self in a feature to kill a weaker champion or numerous minions, take gain! Should they're trying to run away and retreat at the equal time as at low health, you can moreover use you ult (remaining assault, the use of the R key) to complete them off.

Speaking of minions, make sure that you usually deal the finishing blow. This rewards you with each gold and XP, both of which assist you for the duration of the game in terms of character optimization and leveling up.

Also take some time to discover ways to stagger your assaults and use them in combination with some other. Some specific assaults have repute results on enemy champions, collectively with trapping them in area or slowing them down. Take complete advantage of this. Depending on the particular champion in query and the abilities used, this may can help you kill an enemy champion inner a rely kind of seconds. Keep a watch at the lighten up instances of your talents in advance than you try this, however. You may additionally want them in advance than you found need to the tide of the game flip, so use them strategically and sparingly.

Overall, make sure to preserve the traces of conversation in conjunction with your team open constantly. League does have an in recreation chat to facilitate this, despite the fact that a voice software program application together with Teamspeak is a much advanced preference. While League, and most MOBA's for that depend, does have a few component of a recognition for a opposed participant base, the environment has stepped forward dramatically in modern-day years. If you're new to the game and inform your organization of that, maximum game enthusiasts can be extra than happy to help you out.

DoTA2

Next to LoL (League of Legends), Defense of The Ancients 2 is the maximum famous MOBA within the corporation right now. The undertaking play mechanics and substantial enjoy are very just like LoL, with some key versions. Namely, it's far even more complicated in its undertaking play than LoL, and the analyzing curve is lots steeper. It in all fairness encouraged which you play through the in recreation educational earlier than even looking to move up within the path of different game enthusiasts. After this, similar to LoL, it's miles strongly recommended which you play in opposition to the sport's AI if you want to analyze the mechanics and champions. This is the excellent way to exercising a multitude of champions and roles, all without angering exceptional gamers.

Once you sense assured on your abilities, ensure that you're well versed within the diverse damage types in advance than gambling with different people. There are 3 types of damage in DoTA 2: physical, magic, and pure. Various devices will can help you increase your proficiencies within the various harm sorts, presenting you with an area over others.

You will now not take only one kind of harm completely over the course of a in form. In order to optimize your individual in opposition to all kinds of harm, at the same time as dealing the most amount yourself, various calculators exist to help you on-line. Pay very close to interest to the values the ones give you, collectively with the devices that they endorse.

Counter Strike: Global Offensive

For nearly two a long time, Counter Strike has been one of the most famous FPS games obtainable, and Global Offensive dominates the eSports scene for this fashion. CS:GO lacks the steep mastering curve of a MOBA, despite the fact that it can no matter the truth that be a undertaking for contemporary players to compete with competitive professionals. Because of this, the sport requires that you play in competition to the AI first before entering into the multiplayer.

Beyond a few key variations, CS:GO performs like every other FPS discover. The maximum critical distinction that you'll be aware at once despite the fact that is the reality that the weapons on this workout reply to cringe in area of capturing in a straight away line. While this is an extended manner more realistic than unique FPS titles, it could take a few being used to. One way to compensate for that is to fireside in short, managed bursts in region of sustained hearth. This will allow you a better degree of accuracy and control over your weapon. Unless in any other case indicated via the state of affairs, also ensure to preserve your flow hairs at a stage peak. Turn your mouse sensitivity proper all the way right down to save you useless "leaping" of your skip hairs.

Character optimization plays a much smaller feature in this activity, despite the fact that there are notwithstanding the reality that topics you may do to provide you a moderate facet. Pay interest to the gun and the armor which you use. Kevlar and the M4 are your amazing alternatives, presenting superior protection and headshot overall performance.

Beyond that, memorization of the map may be taken into consideration certainly one of your finest belongings. Learn which walls are built of substances that you may shoot via, and the fantastic locations to cowl that permits you to capture your enemies unawares.

Team Fortress 2

Team Fortress 2 is a loose to play FPS multiplayer name that have become at the begin a mod for Quake. TF2 is widely known for its quirky hobby play and pics, as well as its enduring reputation. The recreation consists of over sixty notable maps, 9 character training, and workout modes: king of the hill, and capture the flag. The lessons can be divided into 3 number one classes, offense (Scout, Soldier, and Pyro), protection (Demoman,

Heavy, and Engineer), and help (Medic, Sniper, and Spy). Play styles vary amongst each man or woman, essential to a severa and interesting enterprise play enjoy for almost every body.

Traditionally, gadgets that beautify the game play revel in for your preferred character are "dropped" over the direction of the game. There are strategies to get those devices faster, although it borders on dishonest to gain this. Play the sport actually, and you'll get preserve of those gadgets with due time. Cheating at the sport, on the same time as effective inside the moment, will probable bring about a eternal ban. TF2 is best to be had on Steam, and it's going to now not be clean to get spherical an account ban, ought to it arise.

When gaining knowledge of a present day man or woman class, make an effort to check it at the "walkway" map. In essence, it includes a singular hallway. You'll be capable of study the resorts and outs of your preferred elegance with out the annoyance of hidden enemies.

After studying your man or woman training, interest on optimizing your guns and crafting. These game play mechanics can take a few getting used to, however enhance the overall enjoy extensively while you get the hand of them.

Starcraft 2

Starcraft 2 is one of the maximum popular RTS titles inside the international proper now, and the maximum eSports sport in Asia. The high-quality manner to discover ways to play is to undergo the unmarried player marketing campaign. Through this, you'll take a look at all of the game play mechanics that you want to understand, or even select out up a few pointers and tricks along the manner.

Unlike particular RTS titles, this pastime places a miles larger interest on macromanagement. This method that you need to interest your efforts on your long term purpose: particularly, having the most essential, maximum well equipped army on the sector. The brilliant problem that you may do to perform that is to spend your sources as short as you acquire them. Hoarding your minerals will no longer help you on this game. However, accumulating your resources extra efficaciously will.

Chapter 12: How To Begin A Hard And Fast

The only way to get on an eSports team is to start honestly one of your very non-public. There are severa benefits to this. First, it lets in so you may be part of together along with your pals and create an incredible profession path collectively. Alternatively, it allows you to shape a collection with oldsters that all proportion the identical key hobbies and desires. Rather than forcing yourself to conform to an cutting-edge team, you may assemble a brand new one in your very very own specifications from the floor up.

On the possibility hand, there are actually worrying conditions inherent to crew constructing. Complications and conflicts can and could rise up, and have to be handled as a cease result and professionally. Challenges can also upward push up in case you assemble your team from present day-day pals of recreation pals. Not absolutely every person can be at the same expertise degree right now, and within the event that they have an afternoon system, those present day commitments might also additionally additionally come earlier than the fitness of the organization. These are troubles that lets in you to need to be dealt with very early on if your institution hopes to go into right right right into a professional environment.

Before even considering finding team friends or something else, you can need to workout the enterprise end of walking an eSports team. First, you will want to discover the game or fashion that you would love to focus on. Ensure which you apprehend this game internal and out, and that you're capable of sharing your information or at least in which to discover it with others.

After you've decided to your specialty, it's time to start developing a emblem (at the way to be cited later), and seeking out ability sponsorship. Don't worry in case you get rejected on the start. This is everyday for a crew that's genuinely starting out.

After this, take the time to include your logo as a registered enterprise in the country in that you both live or could be in maximum cases working from. This will assist you and your group buddies to maintain more of your income while you start to earn them, and could prevent any ability criminal issues. It's fine to speak to a organisation attorney or commercial enterprise enterprise help line within the jurlsdiction you live in regarding this.

Finding teammates

Finding appropriate group friends can be the number one undertaking in your new eSports institution. You may be tempted to recruit your buddies and own family. While this will end up a brilliant concept, you want to technique it with a diploma of caution. You want to noticeably ask your self if your courting with those humans can live on and accommodate the stresses of being in industrial organisation and on a collection together. It in all likelihood may not, and this is some factor which you'll need to be upfront and sincere approximately from the very begin. You'll additionally want to have a essential dialogue with any buddies and family humans you would like to go into organisation with about their talent stage and passion for the sport. As fun as it might be to be on a team together with your super buddy, it in truth acquired't skip everywhere if he can't recognize the number one mechanics of the video video games that you'll be playing on a every day foundation. You additionally want to ensure that they'll be inclined to deal with at least some of the organisation stop of things. An eSports institution is a a laugh, incredibly profitable task, but it is also a business company on the surrender of the day. While you'll be capable to tug it off early on, you could't address all of the organisation associated challenges that include strolling an eSports group via way of your self all the time.

There are one-of-a-type alternatives for team building besides your pals or circle of relatives. While it isn't pretty as a laugh and glamorous, you may usually lease human beings. Treat it like every other kind of project interview, although it's an unpaid position in the mean time. In order to find out humans, you've got had been given numerous alternatives:

Gaming Stores

One of the notable options is to take benefit of your neighborhood gaming save. They're one of the fine places to discover likeminded people, and also you'll possibly discover them with a good buy of pre modern records and talent. This makes subjects hundreds tons much less tough for you over the long time. You gained't must spend nearly as an entire lot time training the ones human beings, and their passion for the sport have to be apparent to you right now. You may need to give an cause at the back of your plan in your eSports crew however, so be organized to perform that. Some human beings may not recognize really how viable for them it in truth is.

As with the options under, you'll additionally want to assemble accept as true with with a unique through the years. Relationships do no longer form over night time time, they take time. With any well fortune, you'll short form a running business enterprise courting or even likely a deep friendship.

Online Streamers

Should gaming shops each now not exist or aren't an alternative in that you live, your next possibility is to acquire out to online streamers and Youtubers. These humans will usually proportion your passion for the game and the sport. Again, building do not forget and a proper working relationship can be paramount right here — even extra so than with assembly humans face to face in a gaming save. In order to recruit the ones humans, you will need to be a hundred% effective approximately the imaginative and prescient you've got were given to your group, and be able to explaining it succinctly to others. Should you try to recruit people on line, you'll want to have all of your geese in a row, so to speak, concerning your group's enterprise set up, channels and streams, financials, advertising and marketing, social media presence, and net web page. This can also additionally appear to be a tall order, and it's miles, however each step goes a protracted manner in terms of legitimizing your team.

Job Postings

Should all else fail, you could constantly put it up for sale the position to ability applicants online. As mentioned above, ensure which you have your commercial enterprise in order preceding to trying this. You'll get extra candidates if you seem as no matter the reality that you're already a valid eSports group and industrial organisation than you will in any other case. When you in the end sense geared up to submit, try doing so on Facebook, Twitter, hobby boards, Craigslist, Kijiji, or on gaming forums. Be sure to tailor your industrial the use of search engine optimization (seo) for your cause potential employer buddies.

While they're masses of methods to make cash within the eSports enterprise, enterprise sponsorship is possibly one of the great methods to make sure the long term monetary viability of your organization. Sponsors and teams have diverse duties to a further, which they'll be contractually obligated to satisfy. Just like as within the relationship among team human beings, the connection amongst a team and a corporate sponsor need to be simply one among cool headed professionalism and courtesy.

Getting a sponsor should in all likelihood be one of the simplest or maximum difficult steps of your eSports profession. Some corporations find their sponsor right away and by no means should worry approximately a problem; others take significantly longer and have to struggle their manner to the pinnacle. Thankfully, there are methods to make getting a sponsor a great deal less difficult than it in any other case will be.

One have to also go through in mind that the relationship that one's team has with a sponsor is similar to some one-of-a-kind agency courting. You need to continuously have a attorney or some unique form of jail help gift earlier than you signal any contracts. You need to additionally remember that a agreement is an settlement between parties. If you do no longer like one of the phrases stipulated within the agreement, you have got were given the proper and the duty to negotiate those phrases and are available to a extra appropriate agreement. Do not be afraid to do that. Should any sponsor refuse to barter collectively with your organization or your legal professional, that ought to ship up a proper away crimson flag. You need to think long and tough approximately whether or not or not or now not or no longer you want to go into proper into a industrial business enterprise courting with any sponsor who does no longer need to barter. It doesn't remember how specific the deal seems to be on the ground. Do not allow the promise of cash, journey, or other favors compromise your very personal convictions.

The quantity of sponsorship that your organization gets, and from what corporations, will largely rely on in which you institution is in its contemporary degree of improvement. Like in any organization dating, sponsors need to be glad that giving your organization their coins is probably beneficial to them in the long run. When making use of for sponsorship, make certain to element the accomplishments of your business enterprise to date and the long time plans which you have for the group, the extent of investment that you're seeking out, and what degree of a fan base you presently have and anticipate to have inside the future. Be honest whilst writing your software for sponsorship, and live professional. Some sponsors will necessarily deny your request. Don't get discouraged while this happens.

New organizations are as plenty of an unknown as a few one-of-a-kind new agency, and it takes time to build up a trusting organization courting. Unfortunately, small groups are nearly in no way taken on with the aid of corporations for sponsorship. They're looking to make coins, and they'll no longer make any money off your if you don't have a huge fan base, following, and achievements already to your name. This won't appear very sincere. After all, you may think which you're a top notch crew, and simply need your big harm. Large agencies don't see it that way. They care approximately results first and number one, and few are inclined to guess on a "perhaps". If you discover that you could't get sponsorship the least bit, it could be time to check your programs and your agencies ordinary readiness for sponsorship. Remember that that is ok. Not all agencies accrue enough accomplishments to be ready for sponsorship right away.

You may also need to apply a few certainly one of a type form of earnings technology even as you geared up your employer for sponsorship or undergo the system. Several strategies of doing so, the most important of which might be participation in on line video sharing structures collectively with Twitch and Youtube, are stated in a while in this ebook. These techniques will require sincerely as a splendid deal, if no longer extra, paintings for your thing as acquiring a sponsor. No one stated that making a living off of your passion might be an smooth organization.

While you're working on all of these gadgets, don't overlook your obligations on your institution. Attend all exercise intervals and all fits. It's viable that you can must hire a small set of frame of workers people to take care of at least some of the government responsibilities in case you aren't equipped to give up your day challenge or manage them simply in your private outside of labor.

Overall regardless of the reality that, do not forget that almost all vital groups do get sponsored subsequently. It might also take you a bit longer than you would really like, however in case you actually need expert gaming to be your long time profession, you can't surrender. Continue to paintings in your group, business organisation model, and growing your fan base. With time, determination, and a chunk of correct fortune, you may end up the following team to land a immoderate profile sponsorship.

Chapter 13: How to Make Money on Twitch and YouTube

Online video sharing and streaming structures have revolutionized the way that we consume and make coins from content material material. Twenty years in the beyond, the concept that you could make a solid living streaming your self gambling and commenting upon your reports would had been considered completely ludicrous via the overall public at big. Today, it's a likely deliver of each passive and active profits, together with its popularity as a extremely good manner to boom your very very very own personal brand, audience, and fan base.

Understanding the Platforms

While Twitch and Youtube are unique structures, they proportion a clean cause: streaming video at once to a person's audience. Both structures have been used substantially through Let's Players and streamers for years, leaving many with thriving corporations and careers. However, it's not only a platform for folks that like video video video games or generating on line video. It may be used to amazing effect via eSports athletes for emblem and fan base constructing endeavors. It can even let you get positioned with the aid of a expert recruiter, or to strong sponsorships! The advantages of taking entire benefit of online video systems can't be understated.

Twitch

Twitch is a web video streaming platform this is absolutely focused on gaming, although it has all started out to department out to a small amount within the beyond few years. Furthermore, Twitch has been called one of the number one forces that have driven the exploding popularity of eSports. The commercial organization enterprise has currently been acquired thru Amazon, essential to its economic balance and long time viability. While some distance from ideal, Twitch is unexpectedly turning into the primary preference for eSports gamers, spectators, and broadcasters.

The platform is specific because of its lack of long time video storage capabilities. Users can quality keep their streams for 14 days in the event that they select to now not upload them right away to Youtube. In modern-day years, it has added a partnership software very just like Youtube. Should a person meet pleasant situations regarding content material and viewership, they're able to prefer to have classified ads displayed on their channel and allow customers to enroll in them for a hard and fast month-to-month price. The individual takes a percentage of all of those prices and income.

In famous, users can most effective qualify for the partnership software in the event that they skip at the least three days every week and characteristic a dedicated viewer base of as a minimum 500 people on commonplace. Users accumulate a percentage of the ad sales based totally on their viewership, similar to Youtube. Viewers can sign up in streamers for four.Ninety nine a month, with the person taking two dollars of every subscription charge, with the rest going proper now to Twitch.

Youtube

Youtube has been within the online video industrial corporation due to the truth 2005, and has end up a huge in the enterprise. Owned with the resource of the use of Google, they are the maximum essential video sharing, viewing, and uploading internet site at the internet as of the time of this writing. Top Youtubers, an entire lot of whom are gamers, have made multimillion dollar salaries importing their content material to the platform.

Money is made on Youtube thru Google's Adsense utility. There are few requirements to turn out to be a Youtube companion; maximum human beings can begin monetizing their movies right away. There are some easy guidelines concerning content fabric material however. Much of it isn't unusual experience. No immoderate violence, no pornography, no hate speech, no scams, and so on.

The biggest hassle streamers may also run into on Youtube is probably strolling afoul of the Content ID system. Gamers on Youtube have had their channels close down or their sales redirected to one/3 occasions because of fake claims. The Content ID machine also can place restrictions on a client's account, one of the maximum egregious being a fifteen minute hard restrict on one's movement photos. Should a streamer or professional participant collect a false DMCA declare, this restriction have to efficaciously kill their channel.

Thus, it's crucial to observe the policies for Youtube's copyright gadget, and take greater care no longer to go the line. Fair use is a protection that can be utilized in court docket docket, and it has an inclination to opposite fake DMCA claims. In essence, a use of a copyrighted art work need to be: transformative, that would include announcement or criticism, not detract from the price of the artwork, and not be primary in its use of the copyrighted material.

Most streamers and professional gamers must be included with the resource of truthful use on Youtube. Adding in observation even as gambling have to meet the brink of transformative artwork, and the truth that many eSports are loose to play and now not story pushed does no longer detract from the rate of the copyrighted substances. The best area in which you can run into troubles is the amazing nature of the copyrighted cloth being confirmed. However, it's been argued in the past that the products in those times are concurrently the remark and the aggressive nature of the healthful.

With that being said, you want to consult a copyright legal professional or outstanding shape of prison aid if you feel as even though your Youtube channel might also moreover acquire faux DMCA claims. This ebook have to no longer be substituted for jail recommendation beneath any conditions.

After a while on Youtube, you will be contacted with the aid of a multi channel community. These networks have come into being broadly talking due to the issues with the Content ID device on Youtube. For a hard and fast percentage of your earnings, they promise to assist sell your channel, and help you with any capacity DMCA claims. As with any commercial commercial enterprise organisation partnership, make sure to have a take a look at the first-rate print earlier than you join up with a network. Do no longer comply with terms that you are feeling are unfair because of the truth you need your channel to broaden quicker, or due to the truth you're uninterested in dealing with any claims that you can have obtained. Remember always that a settlement best exists if both sports are satisfied with it, and comply with the terms. You can constantly negotiate with a network, and any network that refuses to art work with you in that regard is one that you have to live far from.

Also take the time to do your studies on any organization that offers to paintings with you. Though maximum in their modern-day-day partners can be contractually obligated to not talk negatively of the agency, you'll be capable of find out opinions and testimonials from those who have worked with them inside the past. Be they an MCN or maybe an eSports recruiter, if what you're listening to about them is overwhelmingly terrible, you truely must assume twice before signing on the dotted line. Most organizations aren't out to particles subjects up for you, quite the opposite. But, that doesn't suggest that your shouldn't be cautious or have your wits about you earlier than getting into a settlement with them.

In most cases, you gained't have any problems on Youtube. This recommendation is in no manner presupposed to scare you faraway from the platform. Rather, it is meant to tell you that the platform itself is going via a time of transition. It is better to be aware of that entering into in vicinity of deal with a capacity headache or perhaps crook troubles afterward.

Understanding Adsense

Adsense is the primary manner through that you'll be being profitable on Youtube and any private net web sites that you make a decision to run. Adsense is a application run through way of Google, and in case you're a Youtube accomplice, you have already got an account. Because Adsense is run by the usage of manner of Google, and Google owns Youtube, you'll no longer should create separate Adsense money owed for every your websites and channels.

Adsense does no longer pay out on a monthly basis. Rather, they keep your coins in an escrow till you hit a nice price threshold – commonly a hundred greenbacks or the equivalent to your close by forex. Whenever a viewer (who doesn't use adblock) clicks on a video on Youtube, they may normally be uncovered to a few sort of commercial. This might also additionally come in the shape of a pre roll that you can pass after 5 seconds, one which you can't skip, or severa banners positioned throughout the video itself. Whenever a person watches (as a minimum in detail) this kind of commercials or clicks on one, you are furnished with a hard and fast a part of the complete sales generated. The rest is going to Google/Youtube.

The amount of cash which you view from Adsense depends partly for your subscriber depend and where your films get placed inside the Youtube set of guidelines, however it more so relies upon for your CPM, or charge regular with thousand views. In essence, this is what you're supplied through the use of Google regular with each a thousand classified ads served in your visitors + how many perspectives you certainly acquired. Youtube/Google itself has been said to take about forty five% of the advert income, so undergo that during thoughts whilst calculating your functionality bills.

Chapter 14: Developing and Promoting a Personal Gaming Website

Next in your Youtube channel or Twitch flow into, your personal gaming net internet page might be one of the finest belongings you've got; no longer handiest for buying determined by using capability recruiters, however additionally for legitimizing yourself and your institution as a enterprise employer. Building a expert internet site isn't everywhere near as complex as it as quickly as end up, although you want to nevertheless don't forget hiring a professional net developer so that you can assist and manual you thru the way.

Your internet site may be one of the first interactions, apart from Youtube and Twitch, that capability fanatics or company companions might also have with you and your group. As such, it wishes to be representative of you as gamers and as business enterprise human beings. Gone are the instances at the equal time as you may located up a easy HTML conceitedness page and communicate to it a professional net site.

Your internet net web page can be a relevant hub for the entirety associated with your team, and for your preferred eSport in elegant. All of your suits may be embedded into the net web page, you can hyperlink to all your social media from it, and you could even sell merchandise from it for even extra passive income out of doors of your occasion circuit. A website is that this kind of powerful marketing and marketing and cash making tool that having one is a bonafide requirement to get anywhere on the side of your team and your enterprise.

You don't ought to do all of this on your very own both. There are scores of folks that may be recruited every on line and rancid that might be willing to paintings each full or thing time with an eSports institution. Websites can be constructed by means of using freelancers, and the same can also produce splendid blog posts. You don't should shoulder the whole burden in your very very own. With that said, you can now not even want to till your net internet web page receives huge in any case.

Understanding What Makes A Good Gaming Website

A particular internet site can be hard to perceive, or even tougher to create yourself. But, once you've perfected it, the variations are night time time and day. A proper internet internet web page will keep your fan base coming decrease again, despite the fact that the content isn't precisely the wonderful right away.

Good websites, and gaming internet web sites are not any exception, depend on one key precept: consumer interface format. User interface layout refers to designs which is probably individual centered – clean, easy to navigate, intuitive, and attractive to the attention. All hyperlinks which is probably right away applicable to the consumer are displayed prominently, and in the kind of manner that the man or woman can interact with them seamlessly with out being overwhelmed thru unnecessary data. The interaction that clients have with your internet web site have to be splendid, not overwhelming or messy.

An example of a properly designed gaming net website may be that of Evil Geniuses. When you load up the website, you're immediately confronted with a big, appealing revolution display. Your eye is then interested in the white menu bar on the top, which contrasts with the general dark problem recall of the net web page online. The most popular and relevant alternatives are displayed at the menu: the house page, the blog, a hyperlink to their collection of movies, an preference to evaluate their current organization line up, and an option to view their current sponsors, preserve, and proclaims, assuming that they exist in the meantime. After that, you word huge, appealing hyperlinks to their social media pages and an indicator as to whether or not or not or not there may be currently a posted on inside the endorse time. Right away, customers are greeted with the majority of the options and statistics that they might probably want from Evil Geniuses' internet website. Scrolling down, you may locate contemporary-day blog posts at the element of recent video uploads. At the very bottom, close to the internet web page map, you can discover a rotating show of the organization's sponsors. At the top of the web page, the Evil Geniuses brand is prominently displayed.

Everything you want at the same time as travelling the net internet web page is proper there at the the the front net web page, with the choice to locate extra statistics in case you need to. This allows the customer to discover the facts that's the maximum relevant to them in as few clicks as feasible, growing the opportunities of a purchaser coming back on your website online rather than locating the information relevant for your team a few place else. Repeated publicity and loyalty for your internet site can help you with logo popularity inside the destiny.

Another part of the net internet site on line's format comes all of the way all of the way right down to some element known as responsiveness. When the display or resolution is changed, the web sites scales itself because it need to be. Evil Geniuses' internet web page is right sufficient at this. Their viewport does scale, allowing you to function their website on line without immoderate scrolling on a cell tool, however it doesn't scale to the amount that could make it thrilling to view on a cell device. In this regard, it's far clearly perfect.

Responsiveness on mobile devices is appreciably essential. More and in addition often, clients are searching out internet sites on their cell gadgets first, before the usage of a personal pc. If your internet internet web page is unsightly, or perhaps unusable, on a mobile device, customers acquired't come decrease lower back to it the least bit regardless of what you do.

Bear in mind whilst designing your net web site that it's better to expose your clients what you want them to remember rather than tell them through textual content. The internet is content material material pushed, and no content cloth encourages engagement more than video and interactivity. This isn't always to mention that no person is going to observe your team's weblog. Rather, it manner that your weblog ought now not to be the number one reputation of your net web page. Keep your weblog on its very personal web page, together with updates on the precept net web web page. Your customers will gravitate closer to it intuitively in the occasion that they need to eat that content material cloth, and every person else gets the content material fabric fabric that they're actually looking for correct now on the identical time as not having to look for it very prolonged, if in any respect.

Your customers are searching out immediate gratification, and it's up to you to provide it to them. Teams and designers who fail at this can locate that their enthusiasts wind up receiving their facts and content fabric material elsewhere, and that they're heaps less probable popular to get determined with the aid of using any destiny sponsors.

It's important specifically despite the fact that to make sure that your net web web page is simple and professional. Don't leave useless muddle in the layout: don't placed pix wherein they don't belong, have an excessive amount of or poorly used white location, or have textual content that is hard to your customers to study. It may be tempting to feature this stuff into your website to "add flair" so to talk, but withstand the urge to acquire this.

Ensure that each one capabilities in your net web site are nicely organized in a manner that's intuitive to your clients to navigate. While you shouldn't assume that your customers are mentally terrible in a few ability, you want to endure in thoughts that the staying electricity of the commonplace internet man or woman is rather skinny. If your clients want to fight collectively along with your net web site to find out even essential facts, like whether or now not or no longer you're streaming currently or wherein, they'll get annoyed and recollect that enjoy after they keep in thoughts your emblem inside the future.

Keep the whole lot smooth, and do your exceptional to serve up all of your most essential features on your clients on a silver platter in your the the front net page. It can not be understated how a high-quality deal simplicity and a rational layout are your pals while designing a net website online, let alone one for an eSports professional organization. The tremendous recommendation that may be given might be to have a observe the net websites of numerous eSport's agencies. Study the similarities among them. What makes them proper? What do they have got in not unusual? What do you like or dislike approximately their basic format? Document the ones opportunities, and attempt to comprise simplest the amazing ideas from those competing organization's web sites into your very very own. It also can be beneficial to as a minimum take a short beauty on simple photograph and internet layout conventions.